HOW TO MANAGE YOUR GIRLFRIEND'S WHITE GUILT

DUVAL GEORGE CULPEPPER

Forest Complex 88 Publishing

New York

How to Manage Your Girlfriend's White Guilt: And Other Horrifying Tales of Rich White Liberals

Author: Duval George Culpepper

Editor: Jessica d'Arbonne

First Edition, 2019

Volume 1

ISBN: 978-1-0913-8532-0

Text & Photography Copyright Forest Complex 88 Publishing

www.duvalculpepper.com

TABLE OF CONTENTS

Dedications *1*

"Let Me Touch Your Hair. It's Okay--I'm A Beauty Blogger." *2*

Foreword... *7*

The Pinheads Of Highland Park Bowl *10*

Decadence At Altitude.. *15*

The Arachnid Toilet Humper Of Philadelphia.............................. *21*

A Royal Fuck-You To George The Bum *31*

The Scrappy Hudson Valley Bartender *43*

Beacon Has Become A Terraforming Project For Rich Assholes From Brooklyn *51*

Surviving Cape Town, South Africa....................................... *56*

Bed-Stuy Is For Assholes... *67*

An Afternoon In Paradise *72*

The Time I Met Barack Obama.. *79*

A Birthday In The Woods.. *83*

Backdoor Donuts On The Vineyard... *93*

One Blurry Night In Williamsburg.. *99*

How To Manage Your Girlfriend's White Guilt *108*

Why Won't White Girls Serve Black Men Espresso Over Ice.....*114*

A Trump-Curious Black Guy Almost Gets Laid In Denver......*121*

Epilogue *128*

About The Author.. *129*

DEDICATIONS

To my little sister, Mom and every black woman who are stronger than all the entitled individuals I do battle with in the pages that follow.

"LET ME TOUCH YOUR HAIR.
IT'S OKAY~I'M A BEAUTY
BLOGGER."

As my conversation with the lawyer from the wedding party concludes and my gleeful drunk begins to crescendo, it takes a nose dive into dark ire when a member of the gaggle of bridesmaids barks at me, "LET ME TOUCH YOUR HAIR."

This is happening at the rear entrance of a club called BSP Lounge in the small city of Kingston, New York. I'd made this place my temporary home, a town close to the city, but far enough away from it to insulate myself from the scourge of Midwesterners Who Bought a Personality and were currently occupying my hometown of Manhattan. Unfortunately, and as will always be the case, they got bored, started looking for a new novelty, and had arrived en masse in the Hudson Valley to condescend once more.

I've now been ruminating over this girl's comment for the last thirty seconds or so while she's had her arm extended towards me, fingers wiggling like tendrils. I've heard this demand a million times from a million different white people and I usually shrug it off or shut it down with a viciously caustic retort. Yet for some reason, this particular instance is the first time it has genuinely irritated me.

2

"You know," I say, my entirely obsidian outfit subconsciously fueling my growing invective, "your request is at best mildly racist and at worst woefully ignorant."

Her jaw slowly drops, her pale arm retracts and her crossed leg starts to twitch like the exposed nerve of a severed limb. "What? Oh my god, no . . . I just . . . I'm a beauty bloggerrrr," she drawls. "Beauty Editor for [REDACTED.] I'm not racist." She sips her IPA. "I understand hair. Just let me touch it."

This is it: the pinnacle of thirty years of humoring rich white kids. I move to sit beside her and engage. "It's a little racist," I say calmly.

"I'm racist because I think your hair is beautiful?" she asks confidently, her left armed coiled like a cobra ready to strike at my locks.

"Well, you didn't think it . . . you demanded to touch it. But 'racist' is an easy word to throw around," I concede. "But there's a—"

"Oh my god we were just having an amazing conversation about this," she whines, gesturing to an imaginary friend.

"Conversation about what?" I ask, my countenance emotionless, my tone hollow, my eyes locked onto hers, waiting for my opportunity to dissect her.

"How annoying it is when black people get sensitive about people touching their hair," she complains.

3

I'm gritting my teeth, but I'm surprised by my response to her words. I've always been aware of rich peoples' sense of entitlement and their capacity for savage ignorance. However, I had never let myself subscribe to the victim narrative that, through its ubiquity, almost seemed to suggest that it was Hip to Be Oppressed. I wanted to resist the easy compunction to believe that humanity was torn asunder along the arbitrary lines of race and that I, as a black man, had no utility in this world and could never possibly succeed with all the socioeconomic factors stacked against me. I mean, there are at least a hundred hashtags that stand between me and prosperity, right? Still, this dope of a girl, this editor for an unfortunately influential magazine, had crossed some sort of red line in my usually amorphous boundaries of social justice and I had to unleash.

"Yeah, well, don't . . . touch . . . forget black people's hair . . . don't touch strangers' hair?" I slowly explain, my usual even, conversational tone starting to rise into the range of "argument with an ex-girlfriend who fucked an older bald guy."

"No, no, no, no, no . . . I'm a beauty writer," she reaffirms through a drunken slur with inaudible cornet fanfare. "I write for [REDACTED], okay?" she reminds me. "We write about this allllll the time."

And there it was: that New York City girl pretentious arrogance I had fled ninety miles north to Kingston to escape. This hashtag proselytizing that, for whatever

4

reason, niggas and honkeys alike were eating like baby food.

"And that gives you carte blanche to touch whoever you want?" I ask, regaining control.

"BUT I WRITE. ABOUT. HAIR. FOR. A LIVING," she barks again. "I just think your hair is beautiful."

"I don't care. I think you're beautiful. Can I demand to grab your tits out of the blue?" I say, the anger now breaking through. "What if I wanted to lick your cunt through your dress because I found your bush exotic? Is that the same fucking thing?!"

"Shh-sh-sure. I guess . . . no, it's not the same," she fires back, her IPA spilling quietly onto the top of her breast and drooling down into her cleavage.

As this exchange occurs, the bouncer, a man of Negro Descent, watches with an expression of delight and confusion, trying to decide whether or not he needs to kick me out. He and I don't necessarily agree on all things, being strangers, him a nigga of a different ilk and me as uppity as they come. Still, my mastery of the art of frustrating rich white girls who think they're helping society, a talent I've cultivated over the past thirty years, elates him.

"Actually," I say, standing up and grabbing my Schwinn from where it leans against the brick exterior of the old opera house turned club. "You fucked up. I'm out of here. If I was twenty-one I woulda hung around and hoped you got drunk enough to want to make out with me. But I'm not a fucking Chia Pet. You fucked up. Fuck you, you banal cunt. You are AIDS manifest . . . wearing a tacky sun dress."

The black bouncer, without fail: "Damn!"

As I ride home through Uptown Kingston, brooding and glaring at people who aren't my enemies, I reflect. I could pontificate upon the intellectualized appraisals of race relations in this country, but that wouldn't solve anything. Cool wind kissing my ears and my vintage Pierre Cardin blazer flapping behind me, I simply wonder: who is bankrolling all these dumbass white girls?

FOREWORD

My name is Duval George Culpepper. I was born in New York City thirty-two ago and grew up in the genteel poor housing project of Esplanade Gardens on 147th Street and Lenox Avenue. Despite my aristocratic surname, my family came from modest means. (Although I'll never understand how my grandmother lived in a five-bedroom house on a five-acre plot of land in upstate New York having never worked from the year 1955 until the day she passed away.)

My father was imprisoned from the year I was born (1986) until 2012. To this day, I have never inquired as to the nature of his crime(s). Still, my mother brought me to visit him on a regular basis for the first eighteen years of my life and we developed a congenial, but odd, Arrested Development-esque Michael/George Sr. Bluth relationship. During his incarceration, he naturally discovered God, which, although it transformed him for the better, made me wonder why he couldn't have found the Lord prior to committing several felonies. Unfortunately though, as of this writing, he has since returned to prison for violating the terms of his parole. Apparently, he bought a dime bag in front of one of those dystopian NYPD erector set observation towers. If only he was a rich white girl who could just have her drugs delivered like a civilized person.

My education took place at a fancy private school on the Upper West Side of Manhattan with the children of people like David Byrne and Ally Sheedy from The Breakfast Club. My friends' had nannies and doormen. They cursed at their parents. We had a great time together.

I graduated, one of only three people of color in my class. After briefly thinking I wanted to join the Air Force at the height of the Iraq War (because I thought it'd Star Trek) and studying aerospace engineering at SUNY Buffalo, I transferred once again to another pretentious private institution: Emerson College.

Still, I never felt alienated from my friends who came "from money." We all had our issues. Sure, I lived in the projects and my dad was in jail, but my friends' moms were popping pills and slurring during dinner about how embarrassing it was that their sons couldn't make their own beds. My mother, on the other hand, was a heroine who once, while running late to drop my sister and I off at school, leaped out of her car to curse out a fat guido garbage truck driver who was blocking the one-way street to the Montessori School we attended. To me, this was black privilege, the kind of strength my pampered rich friends nor their parents would ever know.

Now, a generation of self-righteous hashtag activists from Ohio who learned about racism for the first time in an African American studies course four years ago--learning about racism for the first time--have moved to my city in an attempt to make me feel like a victim of the society that has, so far, managed not to shoot me.

I have traveled the country, working a variety of jobs including owning and running a coffee shop (into bankruptcy) and dancing on tables in Budweiser commercials for more money than I deserve. The common threads throughout all these disparate stories, however, were the woefully misinformed, rich, white kids I've had to humor through it all.

These are the (mostly) factual accounts of those interactions. (I remember them as honestly and accurately as the liquor allows.)

THE PINHEADS OF HIGHLAND PARK BOWL

Stepping over a Mexican man sleeping at the corner pillar of a bus stop enclosure, I approach the Highland Park Bowl for the third time since its opening.

As I enter, instead of a congenial Hispanic man in a bow tie, I'm IDed by a congenial, short stack of a brunette flanked by an all-American boy who sits in silence at a booth behind her. Throwing me off guard, she asks, "Are you meeting a group here?"

"Nope," I reply with a faint smile, thumbing through my wallet for my New York State ID. "Just a lonely alcoholic."

They both break from their faux polite work act and give a genuine laugh. "Oh . . . I can empathize," the short stack brunette mumbles. She extends her arm and walks me down the long corridor leading to the main bowling room with dual bars. "I'm here to do anything you need," she says, immediately realizing the salacious overtones.

I smile and say, "Good to know," and mount the bar.

After I write for a few moments, a girl sitting beside me with a tattoo on her forearm that reads "SIMPLE MINDED" (seriously) leans into my ear and asks, "What are you writing?"

I glance up. She looks like a biracial version of my very white ex-girlfriend. "About how much I hate LA," I say.

Then her pink-haired friend—who looks a lot like Darryl Hannah's replicant character in Bladerunner—barks at me, "ARE YOU IN A BAND?"

"No," I say quietly, taking a pause to consider whether or not to prolong this interaction by elaborating further. I indulge my vanity and confess, "I'm a comedian."

"Oh, you're not funny," the Replicant says and then goes back to flirting with the bar manager of a mixology spot on York Boulevard.

I take a quiet, deep breath and the girl with the SIMPLE MINDED tattoo launches into a monologue, the specifics of which I can't remember, but the broad strokes include the following:

– Finishing grad school

– Running

– Needing to run more

– How good I was at conversation ("I mean, you like, pay attention to what I'm saying.")

– How bad the Sazerac is (I agree.)

– Not voting for Trump or Bernie (She's a rebel, she says.)

– Hating conformity, but really loving going with the flow

– The fact that "we're definitely making out later."

– Seattle

– Needing to get back to Seattle

– How she was a New Yorker for a while (two months)

— "Just relaxing" because her dad told her to.

— Reminding me she just finished grad school

Somewhere in the middle of this verbal deluge, unrelated to anything she's saying, I start laughing uncontrollably, nervously.

"Oh my god, STAHP laughing! I'm serious, I am going to try new things!" she playfully scolds, slapping the exposed skin of my thigh through my torn jeans.

"I know," I say despondently.

At this point, her friends the Replicant and the Bar Manager approach.

"We're leaving, Jamie. JAMIE, WE'RE LEAVING. JAMIE," the Replicant howls.

Then the Bar Manager, extending his hand to me but looking at Jamie, asks, "Yo, who's this guy?"

"This guy is Sonny," I say flatly.

"Pleasure to meet you, my friend. Take Jamie's number," he says while looking away to nod at a random bartender.

I tell them I'll meet them wherever they're going without any exchange of personal information and return to writing. When they're gone, I immediately feel healthier. But as soon as they depart a man sporting a denim suit with a greying ponytail with his frumpy girlfriend in tow take their spots. The girlfriend peers over my shoulder while I'm writing and says, "Oh god, your handwriting is terrible. Is that your actual handwriting? Seriously, what language is that?"

I finish the rest of my cocktail and wish I looked like Charles Grodin.

DECADENCE AT ALTITUDE

The night begins with an Uber ride with a Bosnian driver who makes unclear conclusions about "how actors party." He cannot fathom it and I'm not sure from what angle he's approaching this conundrum.

I'm wearing a Ralph Lauren Oxford button-down, an overcoat, a Rugby tie, acid-washed Levi jeans, and a pair of vintage loafers. As we make small talk, he presses me about my reasons for attending the Sundance Film Festival and I tell him I'm shooting a commercial. When I say this, he immediately flips on the dome light, whips around to study me, and excitedly says, "Yeah, bro?" while I nod slightly at the snow plow he's swerving in front of. He corrects our trajectory with indifference and goes into a confusing story about meeting Steve Zahn, asking if I know him.

This continues for a while until we arrive at a condo in the mountains above Park City. A production assistant from a previous commercial shoot a few months earlier has invited me here after we bumped into one another outside of a screening of a film about a guy who eats eyeballs.

She greets me at the gate with a warm smile. The second I enter the condo she offers me a beer. I accept the beverage and after exchanging some anecdotes we begin the ascent of the wide staircase to the top floor. As I'm trailing behind her, I ruminate on whether or not anyone else is here and what this girl's intentions are. The last time—the only other time—we saw each other I was drunkenly inviting her back to my hotel room in Portland, Maine after the photo shoot. She politely declined.

When we finally reach the fourth floor landing, she sharply rounds a corner and I hear her disembodied voice say, "Hey . . . do you guys have clothes on? My friend's here."

I raise an eyebrow and slow my approach, wondering who exactly did or did not have clothes on. I hear two female voices respond, "No, it's cool, we're in towels," at the exact same time I enter their bedroom.

"Hi, I'm Abby. This is Sarah," a blonde says, standing beside her brunette friend. True to their word, they are both in towels.

I take a sip of my beer, smile, and extend my hand while quietly humming the first few bars of Dmitri Shostakovich's Jazz Suite, Waltz No 2.

***

After a good forty-five minutes of drinking and conversation with no discernible effort on their part to clothe themselves, they eventually get ready and beckon an Uber to drive a quarter mile deeper into this condo canyon. There's a Diplo concert later, but my festival badge already grants me access. They, on the other hand, have to go to the family house of a record producer who has promised them wristbands for entry. It seems benign enough and potentially worth indulging. I join them.

When we enter, a wine-drunk redhead and her bearded, thirty-something fiancé greet us. They offer to take our coats and then throw them in a pile on a bench in the foyer. As we press down a long hallway and farther into the mountain home, I notice a furtive, elderly Asian couple whispering to each other in a side room adorned with World War II aviation memorabilia. When we finally arrive in the living room, the bearded man's Jewish mother introduces herself and welcomes us to her home. In the distance, some one hundred yards away in the kitchen, a lone private chef is plating Caesar salads.

Once again, as has been the case ever since my mother dropped me off at the steps of that private school in Manhattan in 1989, I've found myself humoring delusional, rich, white people.

The redhead and bearded thirty-something give us a tour of the home. I'm trying to get a read on the guy, where I am, and who these people are, so I make a quip to him about the stock market taking a hit and whether or not the price of crude would ever actually hit $16 a barrel. The look of surprise on his face indicates he's confused by this particular negro's knowledge of finance. When he regains his composure, he reveals he works at a bank and we bullshit about numbers for a while.

18

Past the walk-in humidor but before the wine cellar, a man with an Argentinian accent emerges from the steam room wearing only sweatpants that read "COLLEGIATE" on the side. There is nervous laughter from him and the bearded thirty-something couple and then a palpable lack of explanation as we wordlessly continue the tour. On my right, in the den with the ping-pong table, is a guy asleep face down on the couch. Had I possessed a concealed carry permit, I would at this point disengage the safety on my sidearm.

We eventually land back in the den where the passed-out guy was and more people emerge from various rooms to join us without introduction. I begin to put together that some of these people are related while others are simply "strays" who have been welcomed by what I am told is, "a significant Hollywood family." The individual who tells me this finds his way into my Instagram profile and, with grave concern, says, "Bro, you need to up your followers . . ."

I glance across at the girl who invited me here, who is currently passing out while her friends try to determine whether or not the blue pill they found is an upper or worm medication for dogs. At this point, I excuse myself into one of the solitary halls of this home and summon an Uber like Jean-Luc Picard hailing the Enterprise for emergency transport. When I reach the front door, the wine-drunk redhead appears from nowhere and, noticing I'm wearing my coat, says with a wink, "I don't blame you. I'm only here for the money."

I   hum   Shostakovich   again.

THE ARACHNID TOILET
HUMPER OF PHILADELPHIA

As I stumble down the streets of downtown Philadelphia, I find myself in front of a hookah bar called Byblos. Out front, there's a group of three gentleman and a lady who I ask to direct me to another bar called Drinkers. Before the men can respond, the girl steps forward and with a beaming, rat-like smile says, "Who's . . . why are you . . . let's have a drink heeeeeerrre!"

I shrug and go with it.

We enter to find swarthy Greek men watching the Redskins game intently. The first two gentleman who were accompanying the girl have disappeared and only the lone third man remains: a balding business casual who with hair would probably look to be my contemporary. He flanks the girl who invited me in like a Secret Service agent and regards me coolly. I'm trying to get a read on their romantic situation, but there's a distinct lack of chemistry between the two of them.

The girl reveals she's from Minneapolis and tells me of how friendly and accommodating her people are. She tells the balding guy to pay for all of our drinks and our hookah, which I protest. But she insists and he complies.

The girl and I start talking about Ayurvedic Healing and Buddhism. I discover that the balding guy works for Lockheed Martin, which I legitimately find interesting, and we discuss the Skunk Works division for a while. The Midwestern Girl is bored by this and reveals that the balding guy is also an Army Reservist. She also boldly declares while looking somewhere beyond the poor man that she hates the military and thinks it's stupid. He pretends he doesn't hear her and looks at the tiled floor like a shamed dog.

The Midwestern Girl then grabs me and we begin to dance to the reggae music. She acts overly seductive and whatever idea she has of herself as a coveted sexual deity doesn't really move me. Still, she's nice enough and I like the song, so I sway with her. After a few moments though, the Balding Army Reservist cuts in aggressively and I simply shrug, returning to my drink. She, however, winces as he touches her and she closes her eyes, thanking him for the seven seconds of dancing.

And she moves back over to me to order us more drinks. On the Balding Army Reservist's tab.

Then we arrive at Railroad, a back alley speakeasy.

"Do you have a place to stay tonight?" she asks me.

A wave of relief washes over me.

"Well, no, I don't," I reply.

I'd only allowed this weird situation to carry on because every Airbnb request I'd made had been declined. I needed shelter and this was the best option. I'd tried sleeping in the Road Avenger once in Nashville and nearly froze to death. Never again.

She smiles warmly.

"You can stay with me, but I live in a studio," she places her hand on my thigh, "and there's no couch."

I nod dutifully.

At this point, our Balding Army Reservist friend is brooding in the corner as the Midwestern Girl hasn't paid him much attention since the hookah bar. I've done my best to befriend the guy and allay his fears of me trying to take liberties with the girl he obviously adores. I just need a place to sleep, but he wants no part of me and I'm not going to force the issue.

It's at this moment that he stands up abruptly. I think he's had enough and is going to try to take me on, but I notice he's ashen and pale. Then it happens. White chunky giblets of whatever he had for dinner blended with the high-end cocktail he'd just downed fly out of his mouth with the force of a Super Soaker 3000.

The Midwestern Girl slowly turns her head to look at him and then immediately looks down in shock. She simply stares at the ground, pretending it didn't happen. The Balding Army Reservist, most embarrassingly, politely raises a hand to his vomit-lined mouth as if he had just elicited a quiet yawn. After realizing there's nothing he can say at this moment to change what's happened, he scurries off to the bathroom as the bartenders round the bar to tend to his mess. "Oh my god . . . I'm so sorry," she apologies to me. "I actually barely know him."

"It's fine . . . no worries . . . I feel bad. Should I check on him?" I ask with legitimate concern.

"I guess," she says with a shrug.

He returns twenty minutes later and attempts to reinsert himself into the situation, trying to collect the pride that had just spewed out of his mouth. I return my attention to my conversation with the bartender, who's very nice and even writes down a list of places for me to visit in the morning. I can hear the Balding Army Reservist trying to brush off his projectile vomiting episode with a chuckle and I watch the Midwestern Girl's brows furrow in disgust in the reflection of the bar mirror in front of us.

"Well anyway, I'm taking him home. He's sleeping with me," she says flatly to The Balding Army Reservist.

He's stunned. So am I.

"Oh, well. Jeeze. Pfft, okay. Um. Well," he rattles off.

I reach over and extend my hand, "It was nice to meet you man," I try to say without sounding flippant.

"Whatever," he says, slapping my hand, grabbing his messenger bag, and storming out the front door.

The Midwestern Girl looks at me. "Let's go back to my place."

***

We return to her apartment for the second time, after arriving once and then deciding she needed one more drink at a place that was clearly an after-hours coke den. As it's now somewhere around 4:00 a.m., she naturally pours two vodka sodas and insists on having a two-person dance party.

"All right," I say despondently.

She twirls energetically around her tiny studio while I shuffle from side to side like a zombie, doing my best to chug my vodka tonic. Eventually, we begin to make out and find ourselves on her bed where she immediately disrobes and beckons me to do the same. Completely nude with this stranger, she then takes it upon herself to begin giving me head.

After a few minutes she says, "I don't like doing this," with a grin, which confuses me.

I tilt my head and say, "What . . . blow jobs?"

She nods.

I take a quiet breath and say, ". . . all right."

She jerks me off for a while and then says in a threateningly low voice, "Do you wanna fuck me? Do you wanna fuck this pussy?"

I nod faintly and she turns around to position herself in front of me.

"Do you have a condom?" I ask.

"I don't believe in condoms," she says defiantly, wagging her behind in front of my erect cock.

"Ah . . . well . . . I do," I tell her as I lie down. "Good night."

Her Chihuahua barks and she lays down as well, talking to herself about nothing in particular. Eventually, she quiets and we both drift off to sleep . . . for about twelve minutes.

"Get out," her voice barks through the darkness.

I hear her perfectly fine, but instead of responding I produce a loud fake snore. I have no intention of getting out of a warm bed at four thirty in the morning, getting dressed, and walking ten blocks to sleep in the back seat of my car in downtown Philadelphia.

"I don't wanna be NEXT to you. GET OUT!" she shrieks, hitting me.

My eyes open as I realize I stand a very good chance of becoming a headline on Jezebel. So I comply. I sigh and roll out of bed without really responding to her screams. I robotically march towards my bundle of clothes on her coffee table and, attempting to scrounge together some pride, walk out of her sight into the foyer of the apartment. I lean back against the wall and slide down to the floor, pulling my pants on with my eyes still closed, thinking about the misery I allow women to cause me.

As I'm tying my shoe, she stumbles around the corner naked, and quietly says, "No, you can stay," in a soft, deceptively maternal tone.

If I weren't three hundred miles from home, drunk, and tired, I'd have told her to go fuck herself. But I am. I grit my teeth, remove my clothing again, and walk towards the bathroom. As I enter, she slides past me with a giggle and mounts the toilet like a jockey and starts babbling incoherently. Then, as if a surge of unholy energy is overtaking her, plants her left foot on the toilet seat and swings her right onto the window sill. Now perched like an antediluvian arachnid creature, she starts bouncing up and down, laughing maniacally while saying things like, "I can pee like a boy!"

I simply stand there, my eyes half open, alcohol ripping through my system, and watch this horrifying spectacle. Fruitlessly, I try to escape this living nightmare by shutting my eyes completely and waiting for her to finish this tribal rite.

Eventually she concludes and I feel her scurry past me back to her bedroom. As I'm relieving myself, I open my eyes reluctantly and catch my reflection in the mirror. I see an ashen man who is really wishing Airbnb had pulled through. I stand in front of the toilet for a while, before returning to her nest and attempting to lie as still as possible so as not to incite any more activity from her.

Around 6:00 a.m., my eyes open and her vicious Chihuahua, Paco, has his butt in my face. I attempt to adjust his position, but the dog looks over his shoulder, flashes his teeth, and growls ever so slightly. I shake my head at life and its ability to always make me pay for my horrible decisions. I shut my eyes, my hangover too strong to allow for escape.

At 9:00 a.m., I wake up again and really want to sleep more, but I'm certain every second in this deranged girl's apartment is hastening my premature demise. I try to get dressed as silently as possible, but she awakens.

"Oh, good morning," she says with a Midwestern smile that I now know to be the highest form of deceit. "Can I make you some breakfast?"

With my back against the far wall of the apartment, I politely decline while doing a final scan to make sure I'm not forgetting anything. As I'm set to dash out the door, she asks me to sign some sort of "art project" that consists of ripped up pieces of paper with quotes on them in a picture frame. I write, "No matter where you go, there you are" and she squeals with delight. We hug for some reason, and as I'm leaving she curses herself for being late to her ethics class.

I make my way to a coffee shop that serves a very good egg sandwich. It's the best I've had in a long while.

A ROYAL FUCK-YOU TO
GEORGE THE BUM

A few days ago on the 3 Train, while heading home from an audition, I saw a man with a limp shuffle in from the previous car. He introduced himself with a well-rehearsed, "Ladies and gentleman, I'm sorry to disturb your ride . . . my name is George and I am hungry." As usual, most people stared down at their Kindles, Nooks, iPads, or iPhones and into a digital fantasy world where men like him didn't exist. A curated reality insulated from the present moment.

George, frustrated with this lack of human acknowledgement, mumbled to himself and continued his beleaguered procession through the train. Then he stopped and glanced at a bearded New York Novice thumbing away at Candy Crush and asked again, "Can you spare a nickel, a dime, a quarter to get something to eat?"

To which the bearded New York Novice replied with averted eyes, "Sorry man, I got nothing."

George, now enraged and freed from his drug-induced docility, grabbed hold of a car pole and, using it as a fulcrum, spun like a trashy stripper into the bearded man's face and yelled:

"Don't tell me you got nothing. Can't NOBODY be in New York and got nothing. Ya got something, ya just don't wanna give it to me."

I'm thinking about this as I stare at the Stoli-sponsored open bar at The Webutante Ball—a conglomeration of young people eager to cash in on the app craze and bankers looking for a new bubble to burst. I'm no social justice champion, but as I consider a city that's about to spend $10 million dollars catering to these sociopaths, I can't help but wonder how fellows like George are going to benefit. Are one of these "Webutantes" going to develop a geolocational panhandling app that identifies the highest concentrations of wealthy foot traffic? Hey, not a bad ide—

Jesus. And just like that, it starts. You have a two-second brain fart and think if Zuckerberg or Karp can do it, why can't you? You'll lash together a few Indians who can code, an eager graphic design intern from the New School, print off a few free business cards emblazoned with the ironic title of "Chief Hobo Officer," and voila! Every vagrant is using your panhandling app and you're a star . . .

I glance down at the drink menu and order the least appalling beverage—"Digital Love"—as I watch the suits and social media mavens filter in. Out of this crowd, a girl wearing a cancer survivor scarf approaches me with an iPad in hand.

"What're you doing with that camera?" she asks me.

"Shooting for a magazine," I respond.

"What magazine?" she probes, trying to assess my value.

"Y-Magazine."

"What's that?"

"A magazine about Generation Y."

"How do you know if you're a part of Generation Y?"

"If you haven't done anything to contribute to the well-being of humanity," I say.

She ruminates on my answer and her eyes move around in their sockets like she's just been blinded by the Ark of the Covenant.

"What do you do?" I ask, attempting to bring her back to Earth.

She explains her digital illustration startup to me. Something about indulging people's vanity at parties and creating caricatures of them on her iPad. She asks if she can sketch me. Naturally, I oblige.

"That's interesting . . . what you said about humanity," she says hesitantly, narrowing her eyes to focus on the contours of my face.

"I dunno, I just wish this was a bonfire of the vanities sort of party," I tell her.

"Like at Burning Man?" she asks.

"No . . . there was a Dominican friar in the fifteenth century that . . ." I start, but can't think of a good reason to finish the sentence.

She keeps looking back and forth between me and that abysmal glass screen of hers. A series of concentrated, dutiful expressions flash across her face with the intention of conveying the painstaking effort she's exerting to accurately render my countenance on an iPad screen.

"There," she says.

She shows me her creation: a line drawing of me . . . that looks just like the old dude who dies in the Bone Thugs-n-Harmony "Crossroads" music video. You know, around the "I miss my uncle Geoooorge" part.

"Very . . . well done," I say quietly, crushing ice cubes between my molars before excusing myself to investigate the cultural crematorium known as the Party Photo Booth.

"What's the catch?" I ask the booth operator.

"What?"

"What's the catch . . . with this?" I repeat.

"Um, you don't have to pay," he replies condescendingly.

"That's not what I meant, sport. Why is this here and how is it different from any other photo booth?" I ask again.

He tells me something about light exposure and I go in and direct a pretty indifferent stare into the camera. While doing this, he dances around me with glow sticks and the girl taking the photo smiles.

TEALIUM

"It looks great!" she exclaims.

I nod and exit the booth. When I do, I hear a voice.

"I know you!"

I spin around, thinking my cover's been blown. They're going to lock the doors and Eyes Wide Shut me.

"You're from that bar in Beacon!" she says.

It's a friend of a friend from a town where I used to own a coffee shop. Before bankrupting it, that is. We exchange some pleasantries and I feel bad that she's the fiancée of the event organizer, but I say fuck it. Justice must be done and the reality of this tech fever must be broken.

"What're you doing here?" she asks.

"I'm, uh, covering this event, uh as . . . uh press. How about you?"

"Oh, I run a startup."

"What kind?" I ask, fearing the answer.

"It's a sleep startup."

"A sleep startup? What the fu . . ." I begin to say as a photographer slinks over like a poorly rendered CGI serpent in 1997's Anaconda.

"There they are," he says while holding up his camera and flash, "One, two, three . . . nice."

"Did you know you got Meme of the Week?" the girl who recognized me asks the photographer.

"Oh my god, I did? You know at the Halloween party I . . ." he begins to say.

I drift upstairs, away from their conversation, in search of another drink. I can feel my misanthropy becoming more acute. If I don't come into contact with someone who

38

doesn't affirm everything I hate about what New York's become, I'm going to dive elbow-first from the second level of this club into the crowd below.

I glance over towards a guy loitering at the end of the bar who looks like Jonah Hill in The Wolf of Wall Street. Maybe he's got something interesting to say.

"What are you doing here?" I bark.

He shifts uncomfortably, studying me apprehensively.

"I'm not security. Just curious," I continue, trying to assuage his fear.

"Ah," the Jonah Hill responds in a nasally tone, "Just, um, hanging out . . ."

"Are you a startup guy?" I probe.

"Um, yeah . . ." he responds, looking down at his iPhone.

He's regarding me like I'm asking him for change . . . like I'm George from the Subway.

"Can't NOBODY be in New York," echoes in my head.

This irritates me. I can tell my methodology will have to change. This is an LA type. Other humans hold no value to him unless there is some intrinsic professional opportunity to feast upon. He wouldn't be the last to behave this way and if I wanted to get answers at this clusterfuck, I'd have to embrace a tactical maneuver employed since the dawn of time. Lying.

"Oh cool, I work for a magazi . . ."

He cuts me off before I can finish. "What magazine?" he says like a dog in heat.

I mumble under my breath, ". . . ah . . ." and then raise my voice to an audible level. "New York Magazine," I say, glancing down at my watch.

His body language opens up and his dry, chapped lips curl into a revolting grin of decaying flesh.

"Oh, can you, like, sit down with me for two hours and do an interview?" he says with an obnoxious, smarmy laugh that starts quietly but crescendos into a raucous bellow.

"Well, what've you got? Sell me on you," I say with an equally smarmy smile, sipping the Digital Love cocktail.

He coils around my words like a cobra obeying a snake charmer, droning on and on about growing up in Long Island, his million dollar idea for a vague "business consultant" startup, and his adventures in Denmark and Amsterdam. He laments the lack of jobs for English-speaking people there.

"I looooove it there. It's an adults' playground," he says.

I'm amused, but more than that I'm concerned at how willing people are to be lied to. At this point, I'm making up names and referencing conferences I've never been to just to see how far I can push this guy. I recall Simon Gruber from Die Hard with a Vengeance and arbitrarily quote him because nothing either of us is saying makes sense.

"Well, it's The Webutante Ball, sir," I say in Jeremy Irons's faux-American accent, "A lot of money here. Lot of opinion majors—the mayor doesn't wanna piss off, you know."

He nods eagerly in agreement. The reference and sudden change of accent goes unnoticed.

"I love your double issues," he says with an awkward laugh. "Can you like, let someone up top know that I said that? Ha," he says before going on to compliment my work—which he swears he's read—and the integrity of New York Magazine.

"Well, best of luck with the startup. You guys seem like you've really got the right idea. New York is going to be fine with fellas like you leading innovation," I say, giving him a double thumbs-up.

"Great to meet you! Don't forget us in your article!" he says enthusiastically.

"I won't," I say, my back to him, walking off.

This goes on for about an hour and a half: bouncing around to different groups of people who are high on the frenzy of the New York "tech scene." I've been out of the game too long, never taking this monster seriously. I stuck to the dark corners of the world, peering from behind my curtain to see what the townsfolk were celebrating. Now I know: absolutely nothing.

And then, looking down into the sea of "influencers" below, George the Bum comes to mind again. It's not empathy I feel for his destiny to wander subway cars harassing people for change until his death. No, growing up in this city dodging crack fiends and unsolicited squeegee men mounting the hood of your mother's car will build you calluses. I do, however, feel that a guy like him, with all our technological wizardry, should somehow be able to squeeze a quarter out of the collective billions of dollars dancing below me to Pharrell's "Happy."

As the third hour of boozing, dancing, and talking with my contemporaries about their next big app and the buffalo-sized bankers who paid for it all, I realize I'd hyped this thing up too much. It's business as usual: the rich partying.

But as anyone with some deductive reasoning can conclude, the people driving this are no longer old white guys wearing pinstripe suits at mahogany conference tables. No, it's their kids playing make believe in a world that needs a heavy dose of brutal truth. The 1 percent aren't in skyscrapers dumping toxic waste into rivers. They're financing the craft beer shops we patronize and the very infrastructure of our beloved digital culture. A digital culture that, based on these proceedings, has given men like George a royal fuck-you.

Photos courtesy of Facebook.com/thewebutanteball

THE SCRAPPY HUDSON VALLEY BARTENDER

"Any chance you work in the service industry?"

The dirty blonde bartender with tired blue eyes asks me this as I sit uncomfortably at the end of the bar in front of her prep station. The question takes a few moments to process. Odd abstractions come to mind but eventually I realize she's not trying to reveal my "secret identity" as a loser who blogs about his lonely, drunken excursions.

"Oh, uh, yes," I say in what I think is a suave tone, forcing myself to sit slightly more upright. "Why's that?"

"It's industry night. Half off drinks," she says politely before returning to her duties.

I nod and lower my eyes down to my notepad.

The last time I was here, I was bitching to myself about the economic disparity in Poughkeepsie. Now, after the bartender tells me it's industry night (hey, I have bartended) and my drinks are half off, this place doesn't seem so bad.

I stare up at a murder of small batch bourbons slapping each other on the back, laughing and pointing at me. Lexington Bourbon, Bulleit, Knob Creek, Stagg Jefferson's Reserve, Woodford Reserve . . . a confederacy of crows waiting to fly down bastards' throats.

At the other end of the bar, also with a notepad and pen, is a forty-one-year-old redheaded woman I've exchanged several messages with on OkCupid. Our simultaneous presence here was not planned and is purely coincidental. By the end of the online correspondence we shared, I decided I wasn't interested and didn't want to meet her. Yet, here she is. I debate saying hello but my mood is muted at best.

To my immediate right are two middle aged Average Beefs. They engage the bartender with a series of questions that begin with, "What's a girl like you . . ." They let her know that they know she's single because of her lack of a wedding ring and congenially ask why she's not married to a doctor. They shuffle off eventually, one of them punctuating their departure with the statement,

"Sweetheart, I'd hook you up with my son but he's only got a blacktop business!"

The two men laugh heartily at this and exit.

I shoot a knowing smirk up at the bartender and move towards a stool at the center of the bar. I return to writing. A few moments later I'm addressed.

"It seems odd that the three of us are sitting here writing," an Academic Man in his late thirties announces, referring to himself, the Redhead, and I.

"What the hell's wrong with writing at a bar?" I retort sharply.

The Redhead from OkCupid hears this and looks up from her Moleskine. She smiles at me. The three of us strike up a conversation about how this restaurant is conducive to writing. It must be something about the Frank Sinatra soundtrack and the library-esque decor. The Redhead beckons me to sit next to her and I oblige.

***

Two 11 percent Tröegs Mad Elf Ales later, I've downshifted to a light Mexican cerveza. The Redhead has been aggressively hitting on me for the past hour, deliberately placing her hands on my arm to illustrate points in her anecdotes that don't need illustration. All the while, my eyes are on the Bartender, who doesn't appear to give much of a fuck about anything.

"Yeah, I've been dating this guy on and off for like three years," the Bartender says.

"I know that dance," I say.

"I mean, I dunno, I'm just scrappy. I can only date a guy who's prepared to fight me."

Now I'm in love. Not that I advocate domestic violence, but I know the sexual intensity of physically struggling with a girl of a similar stature. To argue with her for months on end and then, one drunken night while watching Sex and the City at her place, get into a friendly wrestling bout that ends with her underneath you. One thigh driven between her clenching legs, her wrists held tightly in your hands like a vice, pinned down. All her toughness melting into a whimper and her white cheeks flushing with blood and adrenaline. You wouldn't have sex then. No, that'd be too obvious. But you would steal a kiss before she hits you in the chest again.

I have no need for soft girls who want to be treated like princesses.

"Scrappy girl . . ." I say out loud in a tone that I think is a whisper but is very loud and weird.

"That's not love. Your Jupiter is ascending . . ." the Redhead interjects, starting into a metaphysical explanation that seems forced.

The Bartender furrows her brow, shakes her head, and shrugs all at once before saying, "I dunno what that means."

A dumbass. A loveable one. Fate had a cruel hand. Me sitting next to this Redhead, the Bartender thinking I'm interested in her. Damnation!

When the Redhead realizes the Bartender isn't listening to her pseudo-scientific theories, she returns to hitting on me. She spins around on her bar stool to face the window looking out onto Main Street and positions herself as if she's about to offer a deeply personal revelation about her soul.

"I haven't been to an OBGYN since 2008," she says with an out-of-place smile, holding her Manhattan.

I nod dutifully.

"You gotta do that . . . gotta pop the hood and see what's going on . . ." I say, bits of my soul riding out of my body on each syllable.

"Do you know how many lovers I've had since then?" she continues.

I shake my head slowly, wondering how my love life had gotten to this point. "No clue."

"So are we going to go for a walk and smoke?" she says abruptly.

Realizing this woman is crazy, I decide to snap a picture of her for the very reason you're reading this right now. Her attitude changes. When I tell her why I took the picture she tells me she'll sue me in a court of law if I publish it anywhere. Or maybe I just wanted to put a Saddam face on her. We'll never know.

When the Redhead realizes I'm not interested, she invites her friend to the bar and proceeds to try to set me up with her for some reason.

"I want you to meet my friend," the Redhead says.

"Why?" I ask in earnest.

"You don't like her?" she protests.

"No, I don't."

I motion for the lovable dumbass Bartender I'd love to wrestle one day to bring me my check. Before leaving, the bartender reveals that she has an extra tooth behind her lower lip. If the night was going to get any weirder I didn't need to have any part of it. Not on a Tuesday in Poughkeepsie.

I shoot home on Route 55 listening to The Living Daylights.

BEACON HAS BECOME A TERRAFORMING PROJECT FOR RICH ASSHOLES FROM BROOKLYN

I grew up in New York City. I had no idea what a small town was until I met a friend from one in college. He was from a place very close to my grandmother's house in upstate New York.

This place was called Beacon.

This friend explained to me that, growing up, it was an economically depressed and violent city. That the quaint

Main Street affluent Brooklynites now walk in search of vintage bicycles, artisanal teas, and bespoke cocktail accessories was once riddled with prostitution, gang violence, and drugs.

But about a decade ago, something changed. The Dia Art Foundation arrived and suddenly outsiders started trickling in, myself included. This formed an odd nexus of "townies," wanderers, pseudo-philosophers, artists, and politicians who collectively fostered an idea. An idea that claimed, amidst the doom and gloom of the world at large, we could design and erect a prototype for a better world. That this secret gem of a town no one had ever heard of (yet) could stave off the onslaught of terrorism, economic uncertainty, and environmental catastrophe. That there might have been a New Town Model, a new way for Twenty-Something College Graduates, Old Townies, the Ignored Hood Element, and the Perpetual Hippie to live—together—sustainably. To live without the pretense, affectation, and wanton hedonism of The Big City. To live without, as Charles Mackay wrote of Paris in 1841's Extraordinary Popular Delusions and the Madness of Crowds, "The idle, the debauched, the pleasure-hunting, [and] the novelty loving."

There was an idea.

But, for better or worse, the gentrification machine has once again lurched to life, sending out its probes in the form of bored kids from the Midwest who relocated to Brooklyn and are now running out of art shows to attend.

They shuffle north like cultural scavengers in search of a new place to make their own once again while disregarding the original inhabitants. But how did they find this place? I thought it was protected. It was just "townie" enough to tip the balance in favor of people who wanted something real—not hip. Unfortunately, these epicureans have had help. Blogger Alden Wicker, founder of Ecocult, (curious name . . . didn't the A-Team fight an Ecocult once?) wrote an article that touts Beacon as an "Eco-Friendly and Romantic Getaway." Respectfully, Ms. Wicker, replication of the trendy shops and eateries of the wildly overpriced New York City is not sustainable.

The article basically makes Beacon sound like a colony of Brooklyn—which it's obviously become. But it didn't have to be. The cycle of gentrification—new money entering into a previously economically depressed environment—does not always have to end with the place being terraformed by people of means. I'm not arguing that gentrification in and of itself is bad. I'm arguing that there is a way to revitalize a region that includes a broader cross section of its residents. The tragedy is that there was an opportunity, a sweet spot in the process, to create something where the sixteen thousand people referenced in Ms. Wicker's article actually interacted with each other. A time where we could have created a Beacon culture that embraced much more than beards, flannel, and fixed gear bikes.

Even though 15.4 percent of Beacon residents live below the poverty line, this isn't solely an economic issue (though we'd be foolish to ignore that reality). The issue is how to create a culture that takes care of the environment and includes people of all socioeconomic backgrounds. There are just as many NRA-supporting, Obama-hating individuals as there are ghetto fabulous thugs who have never and will never set foot in the Citadels of Wealth referenced in Ms. Wicker's article. Why? Because these Enclaves of Cool don't want those people in their gastropubs and farm-to-table restaurants.

It's also important to establish that this isn't so much a racial question as a cultural one. According to the City of Beacon website, "Beacon has approximately 2,400 African-Americans and 2,300 Latinos, compared with approximately 8,500 non-Latino Whites." Over half of Beacon's population is composed of minorities.

Now, I'm going to go out on a limb here, but as I sit in Ella Bella's writing this, something tells me I'm a rarer sight here than the guy with the Warby Parker glasses beside me. I don't demand diversity (which, by the way, does not mean including just a few shades of brown and a lesbian). Nor am I a raging liberal or a militant black man outraged by the establishment. (Between the white women from the Midwest I date and my Billy Joel collection, my Black Card is always pending review.) That said, I hate bullshit and Ms. Wicker's article doles it out by the barrel-aged load.

I love Beacon. I fell in love, ran a coffee shop (into bankruptcy) with my best friends, and engaged in some of the most spirited philosophical debates I've ever had here. However, when entitled demagogues rise to the challenge of laying out a framework for what "these people need," we become arrogant assholes, not stewards of positive cultural change. In this establishment where I'm writing, I overheard a conversation between some people referenced in Ms. Wicker's article and a rabbi who explained, "We need to go to churches and get black people to ride bikes."

I can ride a fucking bike, but I prefer my 189 horsepower, 2.5 liter in-line six-cylinder 1995 BMW 525i. Go fuck yourself.

Elitism. Liberal fascism. Call it what you will, but patting each other on the back because we go to farmers' markets on Sundays and drink beer three times more expensive than the stuff sold at the place across the street does not make us better people. It makes us corrupters who perpetuate the economic and cultural disparity that exists in this country—and the world.

So before you rally the troops of your Ecocult, recognize that sustainability isn't just about prohibitively expensive "artisanal fare" shops. It's about creating a society where everyone can contribute to environmental issues—not just bored trust fund kids looking for somewhere to take their artist girlfriends.

This brings me to my most important question: Hey, are you   single?

56

Surviving Cape Town, South Africa

In January of 2012, I booked the lead role in a Bacardi commercial that never aired. It was shot in South Africa and for ten days I learned about a country whose only point of reference for me was Lethal Weapon 2.

I'm drunk. Sitting at a picnic table on the second floor balcony of a bar in downtown Cape Town at about 2:30 a.m. I've agreed to meet one of the other actors from the shoot for a night of binge drinking and bird chasing. He's a skinny scoundrel of Dutch ancestry—an Afrikaner—and he's managed to pick a fight with a group of six black South African men. Now, to be fair, at some point one of these guys pretended to be drunk and kept bumping into me—aggressively. Not a casual "oops," but a very gropey, hands quickly moving over you kind of bump. I was later informed that this is a common pickpocketing technique in Cape Town. Eventually, I grew tired of the would-be pickpocket's attention and threw him back towards his friends. Aggressively.

This is where our Afrikaner Model comes in.

"Ey, why you touchin' my mate, nigga?" the lone Afrikaner Model says to the group of six black South African men.

With these words, all six rise like mighty Zulu warriors and I know things are about to get flavorful.

"Ey, you don't call us that!" the African Leader commands.

"You call each otha' nigga. Why can't I?" the Afrikaner responds matter-of-factly.

I wasn't sure how race relations worked in this country. I didn't want to be prejudiced myself and assume all whites hated blacks and vice versa—but was this the case? There didn't seem to be an outright resentment, but certainly there was a guitar string tension in the air eager to be plucked. Was everyone racist? Or were children absolved of the institutionalized bigotry of their parents at birth? And what the hell did they think of me—black, "mulatto," or simply American?

I'm squinting in disbelief. Not because I'm offended, but because of the utter density of this skinny piece of shit's balls. He's about to get murdered by these men, but he stands there like a bullfighter. Or maybe he's not. Maybe he knew that even though Apartheid was "over," he still possessed some sort of social invulnerability.

"You don't call us that, ey! You don't call us that!" the African Leader says to the Afrikaner Model.

"Ey mate, I'm just callin' you a nigga, nigga," the Afrikaner goads.

I'm watching this exchange, beside myself, sipping their version of Corona (which they do not have and have never heard of). My eyes are burning with alcohol, my legs hurt from walking all day, and I'm learning how dangerous this city can be. On this night alone, I've seen three random brawls. The cab driver who drove me ten miles from my hotel warned me with a high-pitched David Lo Pan-esque squeal that I might get "taken." Even finding that cabby was a sketchy ordeal: a furtive descent behind what I thought was a security guard at my hotel into a dimly lit parking garage. I lived.

I'm trying to keep my wits and sporadic aikido lessons about me while I pollute my coherency with booze. I run some escape plans through my head, but they all involve me either helping this Dutch Dipshit or leaping to the street below—neither of which I plan on doing. So, recognizing the inevitability of this situation, I decide to hunker down and go for the ride.

The leader of the group of black men keeps looking at me, perhaps showing some odd, bullshit reverence because my skin is lighter than his. This holds weight here. The fairer you are, the better you are treated. It's perverse, but I'm outside the land of the free and the home of the brave— which right about now is the best fucking place in the galaxy.

Or maybe they're just confused as to why I'm hanging out with this Dutch Dipshit.

"Guys, stop it. He . . . doesn't . . . know what he's . . . look, I know him. He's a fucking moron," I slur. "A stupid fucking model . . ." I trail off, attempting to assuage their indignation.

My remarks give the leader of the African men pause. He barks in his heavy accent, "I will listen to him," while pointing at me, "Not you!" he finishes by poking a finger at the Afrikaner Model.

I make a few more half-hearted attempts to quote Martin Luther King, Jr. or W. E. B. DuBois, but nothing comes to mind. Instead, I end up sounding like the Dude informing the Big Lebowski that this unchecked aggression will not stand. I let out a sigh and look wistfully at the street below, wishing I was back in the hotel watching that Seagal marathon I passed up for this. I rise from my seat.

"Listen, I'm getting out of here. You have your Vespa, right? You can find your way home?" I say to the Afrikaner Model, walking towards the exit, not really waiting for an answer.

"Yeah mate. Lekker, baby. I'll catch you tomorrow, ey?" he says with no concern for the army of Zulu warriors standing ready to rip his head off.

"Yeah," I say curtly before chugging my beer.

I dart out of the bar. This weird place. Cape Town. It was not the United States of America by any stretch. We had it good back home. I didn't want to hear anyone protest a fucking thing about our country until they had set foot somewhere as raw as South Africa.

But now I am on my own, left to my own devices to figure out a way home. Between this downtown strip and my hotel are ten miles of shantytowns and economic blight. I'm trapped and the only money I have has white Americans on it. That'd either get me robbed or killed.

As I sober up, my concern about not knowing where I am or having the proper currency dissipates. I pat my blazer pocket and feel a comfortably thick bundle of Krugerrand (South African currency) and recognize that the cabs are being monitored by diligent police officers armed with assault rifles. Things aren't as fucked as I thought and now the strong buzz I'm riding demands I maximize this trip's hedonistic potential.

But despite the police presence, the eyes of the locals scanning me keeps me on guard and all I can remember is my cab driver warning, "They will take you!" What does that even fucking mean? So as I wander down the street, I do my best to mimic the carefree masculine saunter of Don Johnson in Miami Vice, hoping that'll dissuade any would-be muggers from trying anything. In my mind, he is the pinnacle of machismo, but there's a voice in my mind that says no one is threatened by a guy wearing a white suit, a pastel blue t-shirt and a pair of Ray-Bans.

As I walk, I think about life back home: A failing coffee shop I left my business partner to deal with and a savagely tumultuous on-again-off-again romance with a girl who perpetually tormented me. I was in love with her, but she had no need for such trivial conventions. She'd dumped me but still managed to keep her tendrils locked around me. "This was a mistake," she told me immediately after some post-breakup lovemaking. A consolation prize. Could someone really be that detached? It was an intricate shit storm of emotion and vanity, one I was not looking forward to weathering upon my return. Still, I pine for her snarky cynicism and matronly grace. But then those words, "This was a mistake," and her cold glare immediately after she had just screamed my name for an hour while writhing beneath me punches me in the jaw. I glance at the entrance of a bar filled with demure, beautiful women with accents.

Fuck her. It's time to be happy

"Hey, I'm an actor from New York City."

The first group of women I try this lame line on dispatch me with a European pragmatism utterly lacking in American women. They, in body and verbal language, tell me to go fuck off. I admire their honesty and drift over to try it again on girls a few years their junior.

"Oh really? Won't you join us?" This proposition comes in response to my paper thin bragging. It shouldn't have worked.

The smoke wafting about the bar makes patrons seem that much more seasoned and mature—even eighteen-year-old South African college students. One is a shorter than the others but carries herself like a seventeenth-century aristocrat. The second is taller, less properly put together and jaded. The third has beaming blue eyes and is probably the one that gets them kicked out of bars whenever they go out. They're all incredibly attractive and I'm having trouble deciding where to focus my attention.

"What brings you to Cape Town?" the most elegant of them, the Royal Lady, asks.

"Oh . . ." I laugh out loud in my head and smirk on the outside, "I'm shooting a Bacardi commercial."

"Oh, that's so exciting!" they all say at once.

We talk for a while longer as I recline in the corner of the couch with the three them pressed up against me. They talk with a friendly cynicism that is endemic to South African women. It's a beautiful country, but its historical violence and the notoriously high frequency of rape has hardened its fair maidens.

As the alcohol consumption increases, I take a voyeuristic pleasure in watching them take drags off of fags. My eyes are burning into the Royal Lady. She speaks like Julie Andrews and when she excuses herself she marches across the bar like a gentleman.

When she returns, I ask the group, "Where to next?"

The third friend with the beaming blue eyes heads elsewhere as we leave. Now it's just the Royal Lady, the Jaded Friend, and me heading towards our next destination. A club. I'm nearly blackout drunk when we arrive but I do remember my American dollars going a long way. I also remember a girl, perhaps Brazilian, standing next to me in a white tube dress. The rest is conjecture.

"Would you like a drink, Duval?" the Royal Lady asks me.

"Yes, thank you," I reply.

The Royal Lady darts off to the bar and her Jaded Friend grabs me and we begin making out. The music is foreign to me and so is this girl's way of kissing, but her lips are full and my cock is hard so I grab her tighter and melt into her embrace.

We stop.

The Royal Lady returns with my drink.

"Here you are," she says.

The Jaded Friend I just made out with excuses herself to get her own drink. Now, the seemingly innocent Royal Lady wraps her arms around my waist and I lean down. She has a beaming smile, a softer body, and I want to do more things to her.

We stop.

The Jaded Friend returns with her drink.

"I'm bored," she says.

Sensing a power struggle, I Disco Stu away from them and take in the sights of this madhouse. It's a European cocktail of ethnicities you don't typically see in the States. Or rather, they're ethnicities you typically see in the States, but in a very different environment.

I return twenty minutes later to see the Royal Lady and the Jaded Friend sitting next to each other and having an animated conversation. When they sense my presence, the Royal Lady looks up at me and says matter-of-factly, "You're not taking both of us home."

"Oh . . . kay . . ." I respond, shocked but also refreshed by their honesty. There'd be no passive aggressive coy statements I'd need an ancient lexicon to decipher. This expectation of mine was entirely the fault of American Woman.

"You have to choose," the Royal Lady persists.

And the Royal Lady is exactly that. Classy and demure, which I'll take over overt sexuality any day. I give an innocent shrug in the Royal Lady's direction and the deal is done. As the Jaded Friend rolls her eyes and storms off, the Royal Lady pulls me down onto the lounge chair she's sitting in. Our lips lock for at least the length of an extended remix of David Bowie's "Let's Dance."

Eventually, I realize it's time to leave and we return to the streets to look for one of the godforsaken cabs. They're like the postman in Funny Farm, careening around corners with a flagrant disregard for human life. I raise my hand to hail one and two of these drivers fight—literally—over who gets our fare. One punches the other in the jaw and he goes to the ground. The armed policemen are long gone and I'm wishing that in addition to Sonny Crockett's outfit, I had his .45 in a shoulder holster. As other drivers converge on the battle like baseball players rushing the mound, I clench the Royal Lady's waist and slowly walk her up the street to an adjacent avenue, probably more dangerous than the previous one.

Eventually, we secure transport and I'm free to make out with her in the backseat. Table Mountain watches solemnly

65

over our lust and the poor huddle in the darkness of shantytowns flanking our voyage back to the hotel.

We arrive.

For purposes of modesty, I'll present our drunken dalliance in the form of a query she posed to me: Tell me what you'd like me to do. I oblige her request.

In the morning, she drifts into the shower and I use the opportunity to call my driver from the Bacardi shoot and ask if he'll pick me up from the hotel so I can escort a guest home.

"Oh, Duval! You had some fun last night?" he says in his guttural South African accent, laughing.

"Oh hush, Chez. Be here when you can," I mumble.

As I wait for Chez to arrive, I take the Royal Lady for a walk around the grounds of the hotel. We come across a family of ducks and we sit beside them to snap a few pictures. Chez arrives and drives us back downtown where I bid her farewell. Afterwards, we drive nowhere in particular.

"Want to eat?" Chez asks me.

"Huh? Oh, nah I had Chinese," I say, staring out towards Table Mountain.

He laughs as he retrieves a bowl from the glovebox.

"No. Time to eat," he says again, offering me the bowl.

I accept it without words.

This went on for ten days, a superficial fantasy of exotic locations and even more exotic women nearly ten thousand miles away from everything I'd ever known. It was a break I needed from the anguish of my "real" life, but eventually the dream had to end.

It was time to go home.

From Cape Town, to Amsterdam, to JFK, to the Metro-North, to a small town called Beacon, I schlep my bags by myself, listening to "Nightcall" by Kavinsky on repeat. I'm eager to see my friends and tell them about all of my adventures, but I was also eager to see the girl I pined for. The sadistic lover. Maybe all we needed was to see other people, and then, maybe there'd be hope for us.

I presume everyone is at one of the two bars in town and my first guess is right. I arrive, unannounced, and see the usual crowd. Plus someone else. A guy not usually with the group, a regular at my coffee shop, sitting next to the Girl I Pine For. I find this guy's presence odd at first, but pay it no mind and embrace everyone. Then, after some anecdotes and pleasantries, the Girl I Pine For and this quasi-friend/customer of mine quietly excuse themselves and leave out the back door. There's a palpable silence among my friends. Everyone's eyes avert and no one is quite sure what, if anything at all, to say to me. I glance over my shoulder towards a window flanked by a neon Sam Adams sign and catch a glimpse of the new lovers hugging in gentle snowfall as they walk in the direction of her apartment.

My friends do their best to cheer me up, but all I can do is clutch my Maker's on the rocks and glare at the television.

Lethal   Weapon   2   is   on.

BED-STUY IS FOR ASSHOLES

There is nothing strange about New York City anymore. The weirdness I could cobble together from fragmented memories of my youth in the late 80s and early 90s in Harlem held more oddity than the most vivid night out here in 2015. Back then, the underlying subtext of madness made safety in the city a constant variable.

"Take this," my grandmother would tell my well-to-do uncle when he sported pleated slacks, an Oxford shirt, and a blazer beneath a Brooks Brothers overcoat.

"Take what?" Uncle Norris would respond. Then my grandmother would produce a wooden box containing a mint condition .45 caliber Colt M1911. It was my grandfather's during the war.

"Gladys," Uncle Norris would say with a laugh. "We're just going up the block to Sherman's for some ribs."

This was the New York I remembered: a Harlem where a quick walk to the local BBQ joint was a gamble. The crack fiends shuffling across the street, the bums gathered around burning trash cans, and the stickup kids armed with weapons my uncle decided he didn't need. Why? Because he grew up in this neighborhood and though his attire looked like something Harrison Ford would wear in Patriot Games, he wasn't afraid. He had that something only a true New Yorker who'd gotten out of more than a few hairy situations could identify with. It's what gives us our skeptical lens and makes us sniff out bullshit. Harlem—and the city at large—was a place where only the strong survived and the moronic perished in those times. It was natural selection at its finest.

No longer, though.

A voice interrupts my nostalgic ruminations and I'm thrown forward from 1991 back into the present day.

"People tell me I seem like I'm from the 70s. I say 'dig' a lot," the voice says.

He's a lanky jackass of a boy with an oblivious grin framed by a porcupine quill mustache. He's wearing a bright orange hoody that reads "TENNESSEE" and holds a Saran-wrapped yellow pepper. When I acknowledge the out-of-place produce, he tells me, "It's a thing."

"So you're from Tennessee?" I ask flatly.

"Whoa . . . how'd you know?" he asks, seemingly in earnest. He studies me. "Like, I know I'm not ethnically ambiguous, but you are. Can I guess what you are? It's exciting."

I draw a deep breath, realizing this return to my former hometown is not going to be the cakewalk I dreamt it would be. I take another sip of my Maker's Mark and shoot him a sideways glance.

"If you want excitement, go on a fucking safari," I mutter, not especially pleased with my retort.

"Whoa, bro . . . let's wind it back man. I like, didn't mean any offense," he stammers.

I take a moment to analyze the situation to determine if I'm out of line, but as I look around the bar, I decide I'm not.

"I'm only going to humor two more minutes of this conversation, so either say something insightful or get the fuck out of my face," I say calmly.

At a loss for words, he stares forward until the bartender finally reaches him. He gets his Sixpoint IPA and after a few beats of silence, drifts away into the crowd.

I used to get bitterly outraged. Now I just accept these people for what they are: completely out of touch. I don't hate the Midwest or anyone not from New York, but I can't help but get the feeling Middle America is sending its shittiest people to my hometown. At some dive bar in Madison, some tall beauty who can catch trout and handle the blowback of a .44 Magnum is telling her friends from high school about Becky.

"Becky? Oh, her dad bought her a Volvo," she says before sipping on a nondescript beer. "She drove it out to New York. She's gonna be a teacher or something."

I glance up at the disco ball and wonder how many tragedies it's seen. The rise and fall of coke, its awkward return, and then Myself, Jack, and The Magnificent Seven thumping from the speakers while a handful of thirty-year-olds dressed like garbage pail kids—with the manners and decorum to match—dance below.

But I don't mind being the silent brooding observer. I know who my friends are and I don't really need anyone else. I just need to do more. And that's why I'm here in the eye of the storm of Gentrification: The War on the Last People with Souls and Personalities.

"Are these your homies' jackets?" a pair of Warby Parkers and a beard hiding a lack of personality asks me. I couldn't grow a beard, so I had to force low-density facial hair growth to be something cool. "Designer Stubble" they called it in Don Johnson's day.

"Nah," I say without really looking at him.

"Okay, I'm gonna move their stuff," he states, looking for approval from me.

"That's . . . on you, man," I say.

He regards me coolly and settles into his seat.

But it's all starting to make sense—this knot of intuition stewing in my gut about the Rape of New York City by the Affluent, Mediocre, Children of Bovine Middle Americans. Their acquired indignant moral rectitude: white privilege, #blacklivesmatter, cultural policing . . .

Then, at 1:00 a.m. in Bedford-Stuyvesant—"the Next Williamsburg—next to the exact location where two cops were executed a few days earlier, a group of Beckys dance on a stage to . . . I don't know the name of the song so I ask Warby Parker himself and he graciously volunteers to Shazam it for me. "Booty Swing," is the tune. A bunch of flat-butted Beckys grinding to "Booty Swing" in the heart of one of the most notable historically black neighborhoods in New York.

And there's your justice: Debutantes from Missouri dance to co-opted music, guarded by a black bouncer who keeps them safe to enjoy their Kimmy Schmidt fantasy . . .

AN AFTERNOON IN PARADISE

I'm driving downtown on the 110 in my '91 300e towards the home of an Old College Crush who just got engaged. She's invited me to a trendy rooftop party at The Standard Hotel. Her fiancé is not joining us.

I power through the previous night's hangover with a fruit punch Snapple and a pastrami sandwich on a croissant from a filthy donut shop called Tang's. The Asian woman who runs the place is familiar with me and kind. Though when I leave she has the curious habit of nervously firing off too many variations of goodbye. "Okay, take care, goodbye, thank you, good to see you, see you soon."

I arrive at my Old College Crush's place and her fiancé is standing with the keys in the door, about to walk into the apartment. This man, my contemporary, views me with thinly veiled contempt for the friendship I share with his future wife. He quickly masks his alarm at my presence with an amiable smile, extends his hand, we shake, and he says, "Good to see you." Bullshit, cocksucker. We enter together, and this alarms the Old College Crush, but we all equalize and tensions cool.

A blonde is reclining on the couch wearing a cannabis leaf print dress. She giggles for no reason at my entrance. The Old College Crush, a tall brunette with a boyish gait, waddles around the apartment whining to the Weed Dress

74

Girl about what to wear. Eventually, she finds a suitable outfit and we escape the tower and return to the streets.

We stop at an ATM and out of the corner of my eye I see a homeless man approach the girls. He stands before them like a slab of meat and extends his hands. He can barely form a sentence but has somehow roped them into a financial negotiation. They freeze up like frat kids from Michigan getting caught peeing on a side street by the NYPD and I sigh. I retrieve my money and walk over to the odd trio and firmly say, "Women, let's go." The girls break from their paralysis and quickly scurry behind me to continue our sojourn.

We arrive at The Standard Hotel and wait in line not more than four minutes before a long-haired surfer bum party promoter descends the staircase and plucks us out of line. We're escorted into the hotel and pile into an elevator heading towards the roof with several other Very. Important. People.

The Long-Haired Surfer runs his hand through his hair and mutters, "Ugh, I did too much sassafras at the Mandalay Bay last night,"

The Weed Dress Girl says, "Oh my god, you did? I've never done it. It's like Molly, right?"

He doesn't respond. Were everyone else not so stoned, they'd notice the egregiousness of the silence.

We exit the elevator and reach the coveted rooftop of The Standard Hotel. It's 2:30 p.m. and excessively bright, as usual. We linger for a moment, scanning the sparsely-attended social gathering, and decide to spread ourselves over two couches. I sit across from my two female companions. We discuss sharing a bottle of Prosecco for seven minutes. The Weed Dress girl is oddly intent on this. She tells me it's more economical than ordering individual drinks, but I'm too high to formulate an opinion one way or the other. I nod in agreement, but when the waitress comes over I simply order a rum and pineapple juice for myself. The Weed Dress girl narrows her eyes at me, adjusts her Marc Jacobs watch, and lies back. The Old College Crush excuses herself to remove her Daisy Duke jean shorts, revealing her bathing suit underneath, not wanting people to see her awkwardly struggle with removing her clothing.

I'm quietly watching the Weed Dress Girl squirm uncomfortably; only a sliver of sunlight slices between the canopies onto her seemingly already tanned skin.

"Ugh, I'm just not getting any sun!" she whines.

She writhes around, her face contorted in earnest rage.

"Help me move this stupid thing!" she barks.

Hunched forward, watching this, I lazily lift an arm and try to pull the very heavy canopy closer to me with minimal effort. She notes my lethargy, gets up, and with Herculean strength, pushes it away from her so the radiation can better burn her skin.

"Oh my god, so much better," she purrs.

I stare at her through my Wayfarers for several minutes, sipping my pineapple and rum to completion.

"Enjoy yourself, man," I hear a voice in my head say. I scan the rooftop, tapping my foot to the various 50s rockabilly tunes the DJ (a guy with a MacBook) plays. I study the odd confederation of patrons. I had thought there'd be more ironists. Now finance guys, guidos, and tourists who've read about this place on Yelp or LA Magazine have made this their nest.

The Old College Crush returns and with her comes the attention of a shirtless moderately built thirty-something wearing Reeboks, loose-fitting denim jeans, and a roughly $900 dollar watch. He hovers over where we sit for a few minutes until he catches her eye.

"Hey . . . I'm new to town . . . what's fun to do around here?" he asks, one hand in his pocket and the other clutching a Heineken.

"Well, you're standing on a rooftop next to a pool surrounded by women in their bikinis so . . ." the Old College Crush points out.

"Oh, yeah, well, yeah that's true," he acknowledges nervously.

He continues awkwardly hitting on her as if I'm not there. I could easily be her significant other. This annoys me.

"Let me guess. You work in finance?" I probe.

He laughs nervously and goes back to asking the Old College Crush more rhetorical questions about Los Angeles.

"I'll take that as a yes?" I persist.

"Ha, no. Well, yes, I mean. I work in legal for a financial firm . . ." he concedes.

"Shocking. Princeton, Yale, or Stanford?" I say flatly.

He doesn't want to seem like a suit amidst these "cool" people, but I honestly find his world more interesting than the one in which we're currently marinating.

"Come on pal, I can see your class ring," I say congenially.

He clutches it angrily, giving it 45 degree twist and stares at me. He glances one last time at the Old College Crush and wanders off towards the bar.

I then feel the gaze of a Blonde with Round Sunglasses on me. I purse my lips and give her a courteous nod. We begin chatting and I discover we attended the same college, although she graduated about a decade earlier.

"I'm a success story of Emerson," she says with deep conviction.

"How's that?" I inquire.

"I've been working as a journalist since I graduated," she says, extending her card towards me.

I read the card out loud. "Tracy Thompson. Reporter, Stand-Up Comedian, Disco Vixen."

She smiles. "I'm a success story."

The Long-Haired Surfer party promoter glides over to us and slithers between the Weed Dress Girl and the Blonde with Round Sunglasses. He begins, without words, to grope their behinds and breasts. The two girls take the fondling and stare ahead silently as if nothing is happening.

"Wow. You're just . . . gettin' right in there," I say audibly. No one responds.

I feel a presence plop down next to me. It's a Girl with a Strawberry-Shaped Head wearing heart-shaped sunglasses.

"Hi," she says to me.

"Hello," I reply warmly.

We talk for a while and she reveals she's visiting from Las Vegas.

"Oh cool. I just watched Fear and Loathing in Las Vegas for the first time last night," I offer.

"There is nothing more depraved than a double ether high," she says in Johnny Depp's voice, quoting Hunter S. Thompson.

She's won my respect and later reveals she's an active duty member of the Air Force.

"I've always wanted to fuck a girl in the Air Force," I say flatly.

I'm unsure if the comment registers, but she immediately asks for my number.

Some time later, I text her and she never gets back to me. I really wanted to drive to Las Vegas that night.

THE TIME I MET BARACK OBAMA

I was never a particularly huge fan of Barack Obama. That said, I also never believed he was an agent of Satan sent to pave the way for the Antichrist, a fascist stockpiling our guns for a Hitlerian takeover so he can destroy the tenets of American democracy—or any other delusion dreamt up by the paranoid Right meant to demonize the man. He is, however, a goddamn shrewd politician. Just like all the rest.

So, accepting this truth, , what do we do now?

Fuck if I know. But I do remember the first time I met the man. It was for two seconds in 2006 at a rally for Deval Patrick, a man campaigning to become governor of Massachusetts. I was attending Emerson College in Boston as a fresh-faced boy sporting a trucker hat with my name graffitied on it. (I was doing my best to make sense of post-9/11 quasi adulthood. It seemed cool at the time.)

The night before the rally, I was walking home horribly drunk from Middlesex Lounge to my Back Bay apartment. In front of me, I noticed a middle-aged couple having an animated discussion about Deval Patrick. At the time, I had no idea who he was but they kept saying his name with such fervor and zeal I felt it necessary to drunkenly interject.

"Deval? My name's Duval!" I said as coherently as possible.

They spun around and when they realized they weren't going to be robbed, they took an immediate liking to me. "Another well-spoken Deval/Duval?!" they must have thought. I doubt they could detect the subtle difference in pronunciation, but in their eyes, fate had cast before them a younger, malleable, version of their political hero. It was their moral imperative to guide me, a hopeless inner city youth attending a $50,000 a year private school and living in a $1,500 a month apartment, towards prosperity.

"You know, we're going to his rally tomorrow night. I think it'd be good, you know, for you to see the man in person. Senator Obama is going to be speaking as well. Do you know who that is?" the guy—we'll call him Bob—said to me, exchanging excited glances with his wife.

I wasn't sure if I was being propositioned for some sordid cuckolding session or not, but they offered to buy me dinner. Despite my lavish surroundings, I had money for little else than the occasional bottle of wine to bring to a girl's house for "watching a movie" and beef-flavored Ramen noodles. I accepted their offer.

The next evening at the rally, there was a rousing speech met with a tidal wave of applause. As Senator Obama finished, the couple and I began to join the crowd piling into line to shake the hands of the soon-to-be governor and later-to-be president. I wasn't especially moved by the whole thing, but as we neared these two rock star politicians, a sense of optimism and excitement crept up my spine. The rabid hope of the crowd was swallowing me whole and I began to believe, in spite of my deepest political cynicism, that maybe things were going to get better. That maybe Barack Obama would set a new example for what America could be. That maybe this guy was aware of his place in history as a potential president who would be able to choose between business as usual and a new paradigm in politics. And maybe he was aware of how special his presence in the political power structure was to a guy like me who kind of looked like he did during his days in Boston.

First I shook Deval Patrick's hand, and he nodded with a smile. Then I locked eyes with the future President of the United States and extended my hand . . .

And he shook it with all the enthusiasm of a guy meeting his first love's new boyfriend, with eyes as disinterested as Al Bundy watching *Girls*. His general demeanor screamed the fictional words, "Fuck the Doomed," of another Commander in Chief from an equally diabolical time.

A few years later, after college, I was sitting in my room at my grandmother's house watching the 2008 election results pour in. I was flicking between tabs of porn, occasionally glancing at the beaming smile of a man with a complexion similar to mine and the words "PROJECTED WINNER" set beneath him. Then, I remember, a black reporter cried on air because we had finally overcome the one thing that had supposedly been holding back the United States and humanity for all these years: the lack of a black President. Sensing something historic was happening but not feeling particularly connected to it, I gave my mother a call and asked, "Well, what do you think?" to which she replied, "Martin Luther King Jr. said judge a man by the content of his character, not the color of his skin. Your father wrote you again. You should go visit."

I hang up and then go to check on my grandmother, a woman who'd seen eighty years of racial waves crash and subside in America.

We both stared at her television and the mobs of people cheering for joy. Then we stared at each other.

"Never thought I'd live to see it," she says, flipping the channel to a Turner Classic Movie, something with Clark Gable. "Will you bring me that cheesecake in the refrigerator?"

"Yes, Grandma," I respond with a smile.

A BIRTHDAY IN THE WOODS

I start the day at around six o'clock at Lucky Dog on Bedford Avenue. I have a few hours to burn until a birthday party for a friend from college, so I order a Low Life: a shot of well whiskey served with the champagne of beers. I throw back this combination of alcoholic mediocrity that tastes like making out with a girl who's just vomited, and order a second round before drifting back to the maelstrom of irony that is the streets of Williamsburg.

I've always hated this neighborhood. Herschel backpacks, Ray-Bans, and floppy hats buzz past me, dropping turds of conversation about Burning Man in their wake. Still, even I—an equally clueless twenty-seven-year old living in this new New York—was growing tired of criticizing these poor souls. Wild narcissists subsidized by their rich parents from whatever godforsaken suburban bloodbath they're fleeing. First world refugees. A FEMA camp for the bored. Blah blah blah. We all know the score. Mumble the H-word with a derisive smirk and pat yourself on the back. My face is contorted into a scowl again and I'm unsure whether or not I'm narrating this aloud when suddenly, amidst this rambling interior (or exterior?) monologue, a pretty girl smiles at me.

I take a deep breath and commit myself to enjoying the day.

I get a text from a friend instructing me to head to Grassroots Tavern on St. Marks Place, a bar where I witnessed a man painfully shitting in a shared bathroom with no partition to hide his shameful excretion. I'm careful not to eat any dubious street meat on my way there.

When I arrive, a voluptuous Australian woman and a flamboyant black man are chatting with each other at the corner of the bar. There are no other seats except for the one right next to them. I sit. When I do, they keep glancing and making obvious gestures in my direction until I finally raise a brow and ask, "What?"

"We love your hair," she says.

"Thanks . . . I made it myself," I reply in a near whisper.

They laugh and the man talks about how he wishes he had my hair.

"What's your background?" he asks.

"Oh I dunno, black? American? Human?" I respond.

"No . . ." he says in a high-pitched, effeminate voice. "I'm full negro. What's your mix?"

"I'm pretty negro," I respond flatly.

A drunkard in the corner glances over from the TV screen and I glance back at him.

"What? You don't like the word 'negro'?" I ask him.

The man smiles slowly, the alcohol delaying my words' voyage to his cerebral cortex, and answers, "No man, just sounds like fun over in your corner of the bar," and goes back to staring at the Yankees game.

I return my eyes to the interracial duo.

"I'm from fucking Antigua man, I dunno."

"You look like a tourist," the Australian says sarcastically.

"I'm on a safari looking at what all you strangers have done to my city. Go the fuck home!" I yell.

The Australian and the flamboyant man enjoy this and laugh heartily. She goes on to make fun of my camera and makes me follow her on Instagram.

We chat a while longer and the thick Australian makes some comment about sucking cock that turns me on. Eventually, my friend arrives and we throw some anecdotes back and forth about living in the city. I finish my beverage and head back to Williamsburg for the birthday party I'm killing time waiting for.

I've been a miserable, misanthropic wretch as of late, but I find walking around downtown with the temperature at a scientifically even seventy-five degrees calming. Though, when I get back on the train and watch the entire car clutching their iPhones with Koresh-like reverence, my acrimony returns, reminding me that as enjoyable as the city can be, there is still something dubious happening to humanity at the hands of digital culture.

Then another cute girl smirks at me and I say out loud, "Ah, fuck it."

I meet up with my friend Andy, whose job in life has been to keep me from going off the rails when alcohol is involved. Or rather, he reminds me that there are rails, points them out to me, and I still crash the train anyway.

We grab a quick bite at a Thai restaurant whose pad kee mao tastes the same as pad kee mao anywhere else and then head to The Woods, a bar with a humorously antagonistic staff. We drift towards the outside patio and see the birthday girl, a friend from college who keeps getting more beautiful every time I see her. We introduce ourselves to her friends and one of them subtly states that I'm handsome. I literally blush and smile uncontrollably. It has been a long time since a girl has actively hit on me.

I stand on a platform surrounding a tree to get a better angle for snapping a picture of the girls, and one of the bouncers (who must be part of some Williamsburg angry black bouncers union) gives me a "Nigga, iz u serious?" glare and I step off it with an apologetic shrug.

Having run out of things to say to the girl who complimented me, I chug two vodka tonics within a few minutes and drift around to groups of other women I don't know, asking if I can take their pictures.

"Do you mind?" I ask two Spaniards and a Germanic girl.

"What is for?" one of the Spaniards demands.

"Oh I dunno. Is for me," I reply.

They relent and I snap their photo.

Andy and I drift around, making more idle conversation with the other patrons until he says to me, "Those girls over there keep pointing at you," and immediately I'm in front of yet another contingent of pretty young things.

"Mind if I take your picture?"

"Sure," the brunette says in an Australian accent. Yes, another Australian.

Rounding the corner of my fourth vodka tonic, the sequence of events becomes jumbled, but I remember discussing racism in Australia with them.

"Yeah, mate. They'd fucking hate you," their male companion says with an oddly genuine smile.

"Really?" I ask.

"Yeah. Well," the Australian male companion says between sips of PBR, "Do ya like surfing?"

"Sure," I say.

"Do ya like smoking bud?"

"Sure," I say with a shrug.

"Well then you'd probably be fine," he confirms with that genuine smile. This confuses me and I glance over to the two girls.

"We really like black guys," the brunette says.

"Oh," I say with dutiful nod.

The brunette Australian and I drift around until I eventually make the decision to just kiss her. She kisses me back and says she'd kiss me more if her mate wasn't standing right there. Which I suppose makes sense, but the booze has gotten me to my depressed and emotional state so I take it way more personally than I should.

At this point, Andy's long gone and I'm sensing nothing spectacular is going to happen with this Australian. I excuse myself and wander around in search of something else stimulating to do, but there's nothing. I glance across the bar and notice the Australian talking to a group of enamored black guys who are . . . well . . . "full negro," as my flamboyant compatriot from earlier in the evening would describe them.

I finish my final vodka tonic, sigh, and make my way back to Andy's place. In the morning, I feel like shit.

BACKDOOR DONUTS ON THE VINEYARD

While drunk and stoned I am struck with the desire for something sugary.

I am lying on the king-sized bed in the master bedroom of my Uncle's summer home in Martha's Vineyard. I'd phoned him about wanting to use the house for a weekend and he agreed.

As a child, I would come here with my family for a yearly reunion of sorts to enjoy wholesome bonding experiences. Experiences I hadn't had in quite some time. Now, I'd turned the place into a yuppie dreamscape I occupied with four platonic girl friends, one of who I used to date, but had dumped me a few months earlier. After some wildly immature actions on my part, we were beginning to be friends again. Still, I harbored adoration for her and spent most of my conscious moments trying to concoct schemes to win her back, as was the healthy thing to do. Right?

"Who wants ice cream?" I proclaim.

Behind me, the girls are cuddled against one another, glued to the television, alternating between a reality TV program about jail (aptly called Jail) and a Jean-Claude Van Damme film. After some inaudible whispers and the occasional giggle, they decide that yes, ice cream is a good idea.

"Anyone want to come with me?" I ask, staring directly at my Old Lover as if no one else is in the room.

She obliges (probably out of pity) and we scurry downstairs into my mother's Mercedes-Benz C-Class. The Old Lover is wearing her pajamas—a white two-piece outfit with pink trim, perhaps adorned with teddy bears. I don't have the gall to inspect it at close range. I'm wearing Adidas tracksuit pants, Cole Haan penny loafers, a loose-fitting patchwork sweater, and a Kenneth Cole watch with a metal band.

I pop the car into reverse, launch out of the driveway, and begin flying down the dark roads of Oak Bluffs at eighty miles per hour. I tempt fate, throwing the German sedan around the winding roads of Martha's Vineyard while riding more than a mild buzz. I glance over at the Old Lover and I can tell from her neutral facial expression that she is not amused by my aggressive cornering. I acknowledge this and turn the music up to smooth over the tension. I had a mix CD that consisted "Loungin (Who Do Ya Luv)" by LL Cool J featuring Total and Huey Lewis's "If This Is It." I tend to lay it on thick with girls. Emotional subtlety was never my strong suit. Still isn't.

We pull into town and I begin scanning the immediate area for a dispensary of delicious.

"I'll be right back," I say, putting the car into park and stepping out to search the area.

I turn a corner and discovered Back Door Donuts—which is exactly what it sounds like. Well, maybe it's not what it sounds like. Between the hours of 7:30 p.m. and 12:58 a.m., you can indulge your waspy sweet tooth with "hot, fresh apple fritters, cinnamon rolls, donuts, and croissants." I opt for the apple fritter topped with ice cream, which is an enormous plate of diabetic indulgence I am sure will satisfy the harem of girls I have waiting for me back at my uncle's place.

I start back to the car and my ex, but when I turn the corner I see a police cruiser parked behind the Mercedes and an officer beaming his flashlight at my Old Lover where she's sitting in the passenger seat. A million emotions wash over me and, accepting this complete and total defeat I simply mumble, "Oh well, we're never getting back together," as a stream of ice cream from the apple fritter begins to pour onto my loafer.

I stand there in the shadows, holding this sugary confection, drunk, trying to figure out the best way to deal with this situation. This is probably the worst scenario I could think of: a girl I'm in love with being dragged to jail and my mother's car getting towed on Martha's Vineyard. I freeze and hope to hell this girl's charm will send the police officer away. I'm pressed against a wall, observing it all from around a corner.

Victory.

The cop nods and pulls off. I wait a few minutes before returning to the vehicle.

"Uhhhh what the hell happened?!" I say.

"You left me parked in the middle of a one-way street in the wrong direction," she scolds.

"I did?" I say, craning my head around for a street sign. "Yeah, I guess I did. What'd you say to the cop?"

"I just told him I didn't know . . . where the owner of the car was."

I laugh out loud. "And he just left?"

She smiles and shrugs.

"Must be nice," I mumble.

I put the car in gear, tap the accelerator and we're back on track. We drive along the waterfront, which should have been romantic except that I was going in the wrong direction.

"Doesn't your phone have GPS?" she says flatly.

"I left it at the house . . ."

"Ask those people for directions," she commands.

I pull over to a group of stumbling young drunk frat bros with "Colby Crew" hoodies on.

"Hey there. Uh, do you know which way Oak Bluffs is?" I say.

One of the guys ignores my query and stares directly at my Old Lover.

"Hey, didn't we, uh, meet last night at that bar?" he slurs.

They didn't. The previous night we all went to sleep at 10 p.m.

She smiles and shakes her head, "Eh, I don't think so . . ."

I roll my eyes and shoot him a knowing glance.

"Thanks buddy," I say, slamming the gas down and zooming off, deaf to his pleas for us to return.

We're cruising down an unfamiliar dark road. The fried dough and ice cream concoction is melting on the Old Lover's lap and she is anything but amused. I laugh in my head and curse the universe's constant subterfuge. Whatever plans I had for a romantic late night cruise are quite literally melting before my eyes.

"You're going the wrong way," she says again.

I glance over at her, then back to the road, and smirk.

Two years later, after a lot of tears and yelling, we spend two months fucking each other's brains out.

ONE BLURRY NIGHT IN WILLIAMSBURG

My best friend, who I've known since kindergarten, is having his twenty-eighth birthday at a bowling alley in Williamsburg called Gutter Bar. I'm not really a bowling person (or an anything person for that matter), so I'm skeptical about going. The other reason I'm reluctant to attend is because my high school girlfriend, with whom I got into a very heated argument five years ago, will be there. We haven't spoken since, and the notion of her hurling bowling balls while being drunk and angry at me raises a few self-preservation alarms.

Still, Urban Travel Blog had asked me what goes on during a big night out in New York, and this seemed as good an opportunity as any . . .

I arrive at the venue on North 14th and enter the main room. The entire theme of Gutter Bar is "urban rustic" which is, coincidentally, the name of a furniture store down the street. The walls are mostly adorned with vintage signs of defunct breweries and other taxidermy pieces which supersede irony on a quantum level. It's very Minnesota in here. Ironically Minnesota.

In the corner next to a mini-hockey game, a guy wearing a beanie is texting. Directly in front of me is a somewhat out-of-place family gathered around a pitcher of craft beer, their aging patriarch slumped in his chair and wearing a fading brown bomber jacket. I say out-of-place because they seem like the only people who actually fit the decor of Gutter. To my right, sitting in a booth, are two familiar faces: my friend Brittany from college and her boyfriend.

"The Birthday Boy should be here soon," says Brittany with a smile.

We discuss the holidays briefly before I excuse myself to head to the bar to drink rum and pineapple juices until the rest of the crew arrives. When they do, I give a celebratory cheer a bit too loud for the time of day. It's 4:45 p.m. and we have a long night ahead of us. Slow down, Duval.

We hit the lanes. Or rather, they hit the lanes. I'm flush against the back wall of the alley drinking my third rum and pineapple with the old high school girlfriend a few feet away from me. We haven't acknowledged each other in this small group, although we've been here for about an hour now. I sigh internally and decide to simply say, "Hi, Taylor."

She purses her lips and gives me the most thinly-veiled, contemptuous, go-fuck-yourself smile I've ever seen in my entire life. God damn it, we. were. on. a. break.

I turn away from Taylor and glance at the other patrons. It seems like everyone's getting strikes. Raucous macho man "Oh, YEAH!"'s fill the air on a regular basis . . . almost as if the venue plays these sound effects over the PA system to make people feel better about themselves.

When I turn my gaze back to Taylor, she immediately hugs me and I don't say or do anything other than hug her back. Over her shoulder, I see Brittany get a strike. No one notices and I furrow my brows.

We conclude our game and the girls begin to split off to different parts of the city like the Rebel Fleet at the end of The Empire Strikes Back. Taylor and I give each other one last hug and she takes off. It's just the guys now.

We shuffle to <u>Spritzenhaus</u>, a beer and sausage spot down the block from Gutter Bar. This place is slightly more upscale, with marble counters and copper finishing on everything within arm's reach. It looks nice but the staff is notably disconnected. The bouncer looks like comedian Patrice O'Neal, yet seems to be unfamiliar with the human notion of sarcasm. We mount the empty bar and take note of the apathetic bartenders. They stand like cardboard cutouts and wait several distinctive beats before acknowledging us. When they grace us with their attention, the birthday boy orders a round of bratwurst topped with jalapeño-jícama coleslaw and 4.8 percent Gaffel Kölsches for the guys. This vital combination replenishes the fatigue caused by my earlier rum pineapple assault. I'm back in action.

Once we've feasted, I set my eyes on a group of lively girls. I drift over to them and introduce myself. They tell me they're visiting from Ireland and we begin talking about travel and what brings them to the States. Charmed by their cadence, I drift into what (in my mind) sounds like an Irish accent. It's either so bad they don't even bother acknowledging it, or in my drunken stupor I actually managed to channel James Joyce himself. I'll let you surmise which is more probable.

I make a few lazy attempts at flirtation but their European toughness holds firm against the shameless advances of a Yank. I bid them farewell and return to my friends, who are reclining against a fireplace covered only by a chainmail screen. When one of the employees aggressively stokes the fire behind us, we collectively let out a yelp. The employee doesn't respond to our cries and simply maintains his glare on the inferno.

What's with this place?

We all agree it's time to seek debauchery elsewhere. We pay our tabs and hit the streets again for a honky-tonk called Skinny Dennis over on Metropolitan Avenue. When we arrive, it's packed and a gentleman visiting from Israel is the first wasted face I see.

He launches into a drunken monologue. I'm pretty inebriated at this point, so I humor him for a while until he taps me on the crotch to illustrate a point in his story. When he does this again, I immediately grab his lapel and politely tell him that he's made a judgment error and should reassess his understanding of the concept of respecting other people's personal space. He relents after a few more choice words on my part and I send him to go harass someone else.

It's primordial in here. We're going to need strong drinks in order to survive.

I dash for the bar with the Birthday Boy in tow. He's a good man, a polite man. But I am impatient, and I cut through the crowd, lock onto a bartender, and ask for their special—a mason jar filled with bourbon and sweet tea in equal measures. I order two and we park at the bar to watch the band sing "The Williamsburg Honky-Tonk," which as a premise disgusts my philosophical sensibilities. Eventually, the band gets to singing about the JFK assassination. Naturally.

More of our friends arrive. I've finished my first mason jar of whiskey and notice a frozen coffee drink being concocted behind the bar.

"What is that?" I ask the bartender.

"Our frozen coffee drink," she replies.

Knew it! I nod in satisfaction and signal that I'd like two. They arrive and I spin around to find a squat girl of indeterminate ethnic origin staring up at me. We talk for a while and then she starts asking weird questions of a romantic nature. My friends are laughing at me and offer no assistance.

"I'm going to go to the bathroom," I announce and scurry away from the bar.

I get to the line for the bathroom where a few people are waiting, but there are two doors. Some people forget you can utilize both, but when I go to ensure their occupancy, a sassy blonde in the queue barks, "There's a line."

"Whoaaaa . . . I was just making sure!" I exclaim.

We argue for a while until I see the squat girl from the bar gliding towards me like a vampire on a dolly in an 80s horror film. The situation here is deteriorating rapidly.

About half an hour later I get an unexpected text from Taylor, the girl who hasn't spoken to me in five years. I doubt my comrades can handle any more birthday drinking anyway, so I tell the team I'm heading off. Taylor lives in Manhattan, so I make my way to the L Train, which is packed full of fellow night owls either switching venues or making their way home. Being a stand-up comic who hasn't gotten to an open mic in a while, I take the opportunity to do my set for my fellow passengers. However, in my compromised state I feel it necessary to record them confirming that they do not think I'm homeless. It was split fifty-fifty.

I disembark at Union Square and run into Whole Foods for unappetizing, prepackaged sushi. I'm waiting in line underneath a display that indicates when we can advance to the cashier. I glance over to the couple beside me and say, "Is this not the most Orwellian consumer experience in the world?" They nod sheepishly and a monotone female voice commands me to approach the register.

I'm back out on the street walking and eating the sushi which, it turns out, is very dry. When I pass a homeless man on the corner of 4th Avenue, I offer him what I didn't finish.

"It's totally fine, I just didn't want to finish it. I mean, it's not great, but it's totally edible," I reassure him.

His viciously cracked-out female companion, her pale skin burning red and eyes clenched shut screams, "Is this gonna kill us?!"

I think to myself, no. The sushi won't.

I get to Taylor's apartment a few blocks away. It's the sort of place a fifty-six-year-old woman of means would live. We go to her roof and reminisce about high school and a friend of ours who was recently featured in the paper for identity theft. I'd hated this town for a while. I'd felt it had been lost to the gentrification and artisanal fare crowd. Still, as I look from her rooftop up towards Times Square, I realize you can fix anything . . . if you're patient enough.

HOW TO MANAGE YOUR GIRLFRIEND'S WHITE GUILT

Leslie is from Chapel Hill, North Carolina. She's the kind of girl who'd attended an actual debutante ball growing up ("just for show," she insisted). After graduating from Brown and spending a year abroad volunteering in a rural community in Nicaragua that would probably have been fine without her help, she moved to New York City to teach public school.

After chatting on OkCupid for a week or so, we've decided to meet up at a bar and see if our real-life banter can match the witty potency of its digital equivalent. So far, it translates. She's beautiful, a brunette. We've been riding that good-first-date high for twenty minutes or so when, emboldened, I take Leslie's hands in my own. She quickly snatches them back, eyes averted.

"I'm sorry . . ." I say, having apparently crossed some line I couldn't perceive.

"No, it's not you. I just have . . ." she says as her hands fall to her thighs and she rubs them against her dress, " . . . sweaty palms. It's a thing."

"You ruined a perfectly good romantic moment because of sweaty palms?" I howl, both of us now laughing. "Give me those," I demand with a grin, reaching underneath the table to feel what, I now realize, are in fact some very moist mitts. But the mood is reset. We're in tune with one another again.

"So what do you do for work?" I ask, pulling back instinctively to just hold the tips of her fingers.

"Teaching, mostly," she says. "Seventh grade English. But I also help them with their internalized racism."

At this, I release her fingers. "Their what?" I ask, now going for my deconstructed tequila sunrise.

"Oh like, you know, like if a black person straightens their hair it's because they have issues of self-loathing and resent their culture," she says with an eerily cheerful smile. (And all this time I thought I did that in high school to look like Lando Calrissian.)

I take a deep breath. I grew up around black women who straightened their hair. They seemed happy when they were doing it. I remember the way they used to bond while performing this ritual before going out to catch a long-forgotten R&B act play in a part of the city not even the gentrifiers would dare explore. Or the way my little sister would perch on the couch watching The Mummy Returns on AMC while my mother stood behind her with a flatiron, getting her ready for Thanksgiving supper. The "hair debate" was new to me—my family of very black people never seemed to have any issues with it. It seemed to be just college-educated white kids who did.

"What about when you vacation in Barbados and pay one of the natives to spin those locks of yours into a braid?" I probe. "Is that internalized racism?"

"That's a little different," she says.

"Why?" I ask.

Leslie squirms like the replicant in the beginning of Blade Runner being asked about the turtle flipped on its back, and I realize the more I prolong this line of questioning, the likelier it is that I'll be jerking off this evening, so, at the expense of intellectual inquiry, I let it go.

"So, how do you get along with your students?" I ask.

"Well, you know, they can be . . . challenging . . . at times," she says, the skin beneath her left eye contorting viciously. "But they're good kids."

"Where do you teach again?" I ask.

"Off the Grand Concourse," she says.

"God damn. Do you carry a 9mm in your purse?" I say with an inflection that involuntarily recalls the great Garrett Morris.

"That's really offensive," she replies, brushing a few locks of hair behind her ear.

"No, it's not. That's a fucking horrible neighborhood."

"You don't know what it's like for my kids."

"Leslie, I grew up four blocks away from where you teach."

"Well, but . . ." she starts. I can feel her trying to make sense of me. "You're different. You probably went to private school," she says desperately.

I give my lower lip what I hope appears to be a flirtatious bite in an attempt to keep my face from fully telegraphing my ire. It's been a while since I've been out with someone who shares my love of that Netflix show with Idris Elba in it, and I'm tired of watching it alone. I consider changing the subject, but isn't this the point of dating someone from an Ivy League school? Spirited debate?

"And that disqualifies me from commenting on my own race?"

I'm looking at her, studying the way her idealistic conviction seems to be coming into conflict with her proprietary southernness and her attraction to me. I feel a little bad, to be honest, but I'm tired of dealing with these wildly slanted perceptions. After a pregnant pause of a good ten seconds, she speaks again.

"No, I mean, but don't you agree that white patriarchy makes it practically impossible for at-risk youth to succeed in our country?" she asks hopefully.

"'At-risk youth' . . . ?" I start quietly. "You mean . . . black people?"

She flinches a bit. "You don't think the odds are stacked against minorities in this country?" she offers quietly.

"Of course . . ." I say slowly. "But I just think it's more constructive to focus on the positive things the black

113

community has at its disposal rather than perpetuate a compounding victim narrative that makes a group of people think they're doomed before they even try to achieve success."

This date-turned-Senate-hearing drags on, and in spite of how painfully awkward it gets, Leslie never wavers or wants to change the subject. I respect her for this. Even I have my limits for social discomfort, though, and eventually, recognizing the need for some sort of peace offering, I flag down our waiter and order two shots of Maker's. The whiskey arrives and we reluctantly raise our glasses, both of us genuinely unsure whether we hate each other.

"I want to like you, Duval," she says in earnest.

"It's all right. Most people don't," I say. "Cheers."

Surprisingly, she invites me back to her place in Bed-Stuy, and I oblige her. When we arrive, her roommate is eating instant macaroni and cheese in the living room. She grimaces and says nothing. Leslie rolls her eyes at me, pours two glasses of water, and leads me into her bedroom, where we have a very adult conversation about STDs (we've both been tested and are clean). Then she asks me about my knowledge of essential oils. I nod at everything she says until we're both naked and having sex slathered in coconut oil. Afterward she suggests we check out Netflix.

"Unbreakable Kimmy Schmidt?" she asks.

I groan.

"What's wrong with Kimmy Schmidt?"

"Well, other than being more racist than Trump . . ." I say, already starting to gather my belongings.

"Seriously?" she says sharply.

We date for another month and a half. I find I enjoy seeing how deeply I can offend someone's sensibilities while maintaining a level of mutual attraction. Several weeks into our relationship, she goes off to Boston to finish her Ph.D. in political science at Harvard. The relationship wouldn't meet its formal death, however, until the weekend I visit from New York, fail to respond to her texts quickly enough, and am told I "should find somewhere else to sleep tonight."

And so I do, crashing at an eighty-degree angle in the driver's seat of my 1995 BMW 525i, clutching my bomber jacket for warmth as the rain falls in the parking lot behind the Harvard graduate student residences, hoping the Cambridge police cruiser sitting across the parking lot won't notice me. Late that night, twisting uncomfortably in my bucket seat, I find myself screaming out loud, "I thought you wanted to help my people get off the streets!"

The campus cop doesn't seem to notice a thing.

WHY WON'T WHITE GIRLS SERVE BLACK MEN ESPRESSO OVER ICE

Attempting to break my caffeine routine, I decide to try a new coffee shop I've heard about: The neatly tucked away

[REDACTED] located in an area of Kingston, NY that was previously unknown to me—but shouldn't have been.

Its geographic location would technically be considered "Midtown" Kingston—a place simultaneously lauded for its potential dangers and fabulous under market value real estate deals. However, like that level in Super Mario Bros. 3 where you can crouch and slide behind the level's backdrop, this area is conspicuously separated from people that would likely be unable to afford the area's commercial offerings. Though if you follow a magical bridge that goes Over the Niggers and Through the Woods, to The New Coffee Shop We Go…a hidden path will appear, leading new affluent upstate homeowners to an effigy of the excess they'd just escaped.

Cruising down this road in my '92 5-Series, parallel to the proverbial railroad tracks, I pass a sensory deprivation tank facility and find myself at a dead end. I glance around for a moment, not seeing my destination, but realize the front facade is blocked by a black Range Rover a girl dressed like Huckleberry Finn is loading produce into. I sigh and enter.

As I approach the counter, a girl with a habitat for humanity t-shirt floats past me towards the exit and I order an espresso over ice from a bearded Australian gentleman with Warby Parkers on. He first places the ice into a cup the size of a thimble and realizes it may be too small.

"Probably need a larger glass, eh?" he asks.

I shrug and his redhead female co-worker makes note of his adjustment. After I pay and begin to walk to my seat, she fires at me in what I'm sure she thinks is a humorous tone—but comes off like an accusatory shrill white woman—that I'd, "Better not fill that cup with milk and make a free latte!"

This is the second time in 7 days I've tried to order a fucking espresso over ice and had some issue arise—both times at the hands of a self-righteous white girl coffee Gestapo.

"You know," I start, trying not to get immediately niggerish in this quaint establishment. "You've got a pretty bleak outlook on humanity. All of us scheming to save a dollar on a latte."

"I knooooowwwww," she concedes. "I just used to do that all the time when I'd go to Starbucks."

"Well then you're a horrible person," I say with a glib smile, hoping my countenance reflects my inner Charles Grodin.

She smiles back with no eye contact and behind me a man and woman dressed like that famous depression era couple wander in. The man drags his worn vintage chuka boots across the exposed wood floor like a hungry Kodiak bear entering an unzipped tent. His female companion in tow asks how his boat and house (two separate entities) are doing, but the man can't remember which ones she's seen. They order—an orange juice and something in a very tiny glass she sips on like a Hummingbird—and he pays for both their beverages from a large wad of cash loosely resting in his torn, faded Levis jeans pocket. The girl quips, "Do you want a wallet?"

"No…" in a slow, low, lazy drawl of indeterminate origin. "My wallet's too big."

I sip my espresso over ice, which is very good, and stand up to explore the cafe's mid-century-modern-farmhouse-chic whatever table top displays crammed with every possible accoutrement of "we just bought a house outside a city" goods including: Biodegradable food storage bags, organic household cleaning solutions and $4 rolls of paper towels. I crouch down to look closer and confirm the price, disappearing from the redhead baristas view for several seconds, and rise up again.

"Oh!" she barks, startled. "I was like, 'where'd he go?!'"

"I was trying to find the free milk," I mutter.

Nervous laughter preempts, "I thought you were going to do 'the elevator' trick."

"Yeah, I'm out of tricks," I respond flatly.

I go back to my seat at the wrought iron based table with faux reclaimed wood top and ponder the other time this week a white girl had a conniption fit over my preference for espresso over ice.

After an evening of arguing with a romantic interest's co-workers about the Telecommunications Act of 1996 and proper polling methodologies at The Big Hunt in

Washington, D.C., I stir into consciousness. My head is ringing with the cheap Pollack vodka she and I thought was a good idea to do shots of before doing an impromptu Bluth Family Chicken Dance in her apartment. Processing all of this, I slither out of bed to rummage for my clothes.

"Do you want to grab a coffee?" she asks, already halfway through her morning routine, sliding her long toned legs into her running shorts.

"Sure," I say. "I was going to head to Starbucks."

She laughs. "We can do better than Starbucks."

I blink flatly, shrug as I slide my Topsiders on and we make our way to The Coffee Bar.

As we approach, the front outside seating area is a garrison of stoic D.C. white people who sit with an eerie stillness, quietly murmuring to each other in what could be construed as "conversation" but lacking emotive gestures one would typically associate with the act. We enter, approach the counter and I notice "TUMERIC LATTE" scrawled on the chalkboard which sounds appealing. The Runner orders her beverage and I begin to order mine.

"Can I have the Tumeric latte?"

"Sure," the polite young black counter girl says.

"Can I have it with almond milk?" I amend.

"Oh…we only have oak or hemp milk."

"I...don't know what those are. Just a shot of espresso please."

"Okay."

"Over ice," I add.

Time stops. I get sheepish, bashful, averted eyes and she stays still for a few beats like she's trying to avoid a Tyrannosaur and then, without acknowledging me, resumes pulling the shot.

"Over ice, please." I repeat.

Seemingly materializing out of the wall like T-1000, the barista's manager, a tall lanky thing with a hook nose and aggressive Bible Belt eyeshadow, turns around and informs me, "We don't do that here," while scooping ice for something else.

Now, it's important to note that I in fact owned and ran a very successful coffee shop—into bankruptcy—in my early 20s. While it's longevity certainly reflects my business acumen, it shouldn't reflect my knowledge of coffee. Or at the very least earned me the right to order it however I want. However, I'm hungover. It's a Mid-Atlantic 89 degrees and all I want is my espresso, cooled over blocks of frozen H20. Yet it seems as if I'm in 1993's Demolition Man and I don't know how to use the Three Sea-Shells.

"Ok...can you just give me an espresso and then give me a cup of ice. For water," I negotiate.

More sheepishness.

Eventually, I'm handed a plastic cup of ice and my espresso. Everyone behind the counter is watching me as if I'm wearing an explosive vest and have my thumb on the detonator. Bated breaths abound, I pour the espresso over the ice and the hook nosed manager clenches her jaw and closes her eyes like she just lost a soldier to an IED in Tikrit. "Just so you know," she snarls. "We probably won't give you a cup of ice next time."

Can't a nigga get some iced espresso?

A Trump-Curious Black Guy Almost Gets Laid in Denver

I've been on a quest to find that most elusive of prizes: a girlfriend (or simply a girl who responds to my texts) who breaks the mold of the ubiquitous aspiring LA actress or deadly serious New York Social Justice Warrior. Night after night at Bar Stella in Los Feliz or during happy hour at Sweet and Vicious on the Lower East Side, I'd brood and complain to friends about not meeting girls who understood the "complexity" of (an admitted) narcissist like myself.

So, like most people facing a deep existential crisis, I turned to my smartphone and within its cold blue glow in my bedroom at 3:00 a.m. I discovered romantic enlightenment in the form of a very curious Instagram account called @Girlsofthemarsh: hot girls doing macho stuff like fishing, hunting, and driving manual-transmission pickup trucks in places society told me weren't safe for a lone black man to visit. But its alien exoticism was part of the intrigue, a stark contrast to the godawful derivative art openings or shoe-gazing indie "rock" shows I've been dragged to over the years in an attempt to mimic a Hu-Mon relationship. I decided, if I truly wanted to be happy, I'd have to go questing in places that thought America Needed to Be Great Again. The savage Middle America that was home to nine-foot-tall, broad-shouldered, strong white women who hurled boulders into ravines for sport and wrestled bulls to the ground by their horns wearing nothing but trucker hats and rebel flag bikinis.

And thusly, a spontaneous thirteen-hour drive later, this weird compulsion to seek out women of this nature has me nursing a margarita in Denver, Colorado at Prohibition Bar & Grill, studying a trio of girls who seem like they jumped right out of my bizarre Instagram fantasy. A half hour goes by as we exchange inviting glances with one another, but my overthinking of an opening line prolongs the silence and I sense my window of opportunity waning. Desperate, I make my margarita disappear, wait for the confidence to arrive, and decide the most practical way to break the ice is to rally the entire establishment into a drunken bastardization of our national anthem.

Shortly after this, the girls approach me, startled by my overt adulation of the United States of America, and introduce themselves. The first girl is a short blonde, the other a tall one, and the third a brunette who meets my five-foot-seven-inch eye line evenly. They inform me they're on a Girls' Trip from Wisconsin and this piques my curiosity further. Did they only look like the type of girls who existed in my fantasy, or were they the real deal? There was only one way to find out.

"So are you guys voting for Trump?" I ask abruptly, awkwardly.

They all smirk and look at each other before the Shorter Wisconsin Blonde takes the lead and fires back like a spread of buckshot, "Why? Let me guess, you're like a New York liberal? You hate Donald Trump, right?"

I study her and consider her line of questioning. I frankly hadn't made a decision about Trump yet. This was early on in his campaign and the full bore of his dubious rhetoric—rhetoric whose hidden Machiavellian motives I was more interested in trying to divine—had yet to charm the nation. It was confounding because this "new" Trump was a deviation from the one I'd grown up seeing in cameos on The Fresh Prince of Bel-Air and Home Alone 2, the one we all seemed fine with. I had even read Trump: The Art of the Deal when I was a twenty-three-year-old in the midst of bankrupting a coffee shop and found some of his braggadocious aphorisms about business to be mildly inspiring. But president?

Still, this was an opportunity to break new ground and experience a different type of dalliance with a type of a girl I've not once encountered in my travels. Yes, it was time to relish this era of sexual fluidity and express my identity however I wanted and not be locked into some archaic binary dictated by the draconian white male patriarchy. It was time explore a side of me I'd had to hide for so long. It was time to be . . . a little Trump-Curious.

"I'm not sure. I mean, I guess I'm open to the guy if he demonstrates some competency," I respond noncommittally.

I might as well have told her I'm the guy who wrote that "Red Solo Cup" song because her disposition immediately shifts from hostile inquiry to exotic curiosity. "Really? That's like," she starts as she brushes a dirty blonde lock from her face, "so surprising."

I order another margarita.

***

We consume several more drinks and the focus of my attention shifts to the bartender, who has been eyeing me curiously since I walked in. She's not particularly tall, but she fills out her thin red flannel shirt and tight denim jeans with a physicality acquired through work—not the vanity of Pilates or hot vinyasa yoga. Her face is also freckled and tight for her age, suggesting time spent out in the sun. A woman of mountain recreation.

Initially, I perceive her observation of me to be some form of hostility, perhaps even racially motivated, but after she asks some probing questions about my New York State ID, she surprises me with a proposition. "I usually don't do this," she says, leaning closer to me over the oak bar top, "but I'd be happy to give you my number and show you around tomorrow if you want."

I try to steal a quick sideways glance at the trio I'd been chatting with earlier and realize I have to make a decision here and now. I'd learned all too well in my early twenties the folly of chasing two women at once . . . so naturally, I oblige her offer. "Yeah that'd be great," I say.

The bartender nods with a small smile, a deeply intense stare and goes to make me another drink without asking. As she does, the shorter brunette of the Wisconsin Trio saunters to my side.

"So were you serious about voting for Trump?" she asks, hypnotically stirring her whiskey sour.

"Well, I wouldn't say I'm definitely sold on the guy, but I like where he stands on foreign policy and taxes," I respond.

"I mean," her voice lowering, a tinge of sorrow washing over it, "I don't love everything about him, but I have to say I like him more than Hillary. I just don't trust her."

"Yeah, he's definitely a jackass, but at least I know he's a jackass. And I think he knows that about himself too. A dark honesty, I guess," I say with a shrug.

"Right!" she exclaims and pauses before sipping her now properly mixed cocktail, searching for more ways to contextualize this strange black man alone in Denver. "What do you do for fun in New York?"

"Honestly, I just like getting drunk in the woods behind my grandmother's house and shooting my grandfather's old rifles," I confess.

"Oh my god, really? I go shooting with my dad all the time back home," she says, nearly beaming. "He'd really like you."

I laugh. "Would he though?"

She blushes and I glance over my shoulder and notice the bartender who offered to show me around tomorrow glaring at me briefly before returning to her duties. There goes that.

More drinks and some time later, an impromptu dance party breaks out on this particularly animated Sunday evening. The Wisconsin Trio, who I've noticed have had this weird James Franco type lingering behind them all evening, announce they're heading back to their hotel. They've invited me to join, but make a tacit suggestion that this Franco guy isn't welcome. I nod and wait until he's preoccupied "whipping and nae naeing" on the dance floor to give the girls the signal to make a subtle exit back towards their Holiday Inn. A few blocks down though, the James Franco guy comes sprinting after us.

"Hey, y'all left without saying goodbye!" he yells, sweating, panting, and wavering from side to side. The girls are drunk and unable to articulate themselves so they resort to nervously muttering to one another.

"I think they're done for the night, I'm just walking them home and then Ubering back to my place," I lie to him.

"Ah shit man, it's early! Come on, forget them, I'll buy you a drink, bro," he commands without the customary amiability that would make you want to comply.

As a younger man, I would have felt some weird need to oblige, but as a goal-oriented thirty-year-old, I simply say, "No thanks," and continue walking the girls.

"Well what the fuck," he starts, becoming tense and losing whatever cool he thought he was holding onto. "I got us a table at my boy's bar. It's fucking packed and it's hard to get a table."

By this point, the girls have kept walking and I'm standing in the middle of Denver being yelled at by a guy I don't know, occasionally interjecting with a "Yeah takes all kinds" or a "You'll be aight." Eventually, he stops his tirade and bursts into a full gallop across the street into the night and I see the staggering trio off in the distance under the neon of the Holiday Inn facade. I consider jogging after them, but decide I've learned enough about Middle America Girls. For now.

EPILOGUE

Many of these tales were written when I was in my early to mid 20s. I'm now 32 years old and as pompously douchey as I may come off, I hope the point behind the stories you've just read is understood. I don't hate women, I don't hate white women (obviously), but there is a dangerous arrogance and condescension this demographic embodies that American culture does not spend enough time castigating. Remember, the only thing more dangerous to black communities than racist cops are white women with real estate agents.

Duval   George   Culpepper   Will   Return.

ABOUT THE AUTHOR

Dad in jail. Upper West Side Private School. Raised in Harlem, watching *Sailor Moon*.

You do the math.